ON BEING SURE
IN RELIGION

ON BEING SURE
IN RELIGION

BY

IAN T. RAMSEY

UNIVERSITY OF LONDON

THE ATHLONE PRESS

1963

Published by

THE ATHLONE PRESS
UNIVERSITY OF LONDON

at 2 Gower Street, London WC1
Distributed by Constable & Co Ltd
12 *Orange Street, London* WC2

Canada
Oxford University Press
Toronto

U.S.A.
Oxford University Press Inc
New York

Printed in Great Britain by
WESTERN PRINTING SERVICES LTD
BRISTOL

PREFACE

WHAT follows is a revised and slightly expanded version
of the Frederick Denison Maurice lectures for 1961–2,
given at King's College, London. My indebtedness to the
work of others, especially Dr. Vidler, will be obvious from
both the footnotes and the text. I only hope that in revising
the lectures for publication, all changes have been im-
provements. Even then, it is hardly likely that they will be
worthy of the friendly hospitality I enjoyed at King's; the
generous reception the audience accorded to the lectures;
and the kindness and charity of those who took the Chair
on successive evenings—the Dean of St. Paul's, Professor
Hywel D. Lewis, and the Dean of King's College. But no
doubt Maurice himself would be gratified most of all to
reflect that far from being compelled to resign at the end
of the first lecture, I was still welcome to return to King's
College to give two more.

I.T.R.

CONTENTS

vii

I

ETERNAL PUNISHMENT

How natural it is to expect to be sure in religion! Religion is, for the believer, of such obvious importance and of such high significance that it is incredible (it might be said) that God (if God there be) could ever allow any uncertainty about it. But our suspicions are aroused when we recall that historically it has been not Christian apologists like Joseph Butler, but critics, deists like Charles Blount and Matthew Tindal, who have argued that if we are not sure about revelation, it is hardly worth the name. It has been critics who have claimed that any uncertainty about the evidence for revelation becomes 'a positive argument against it', because 'it cannot be supposed that if true, it would be left to subsist upon doubtful evidence'.[1]

On the other hand, the religious man's expectation of certainty may have arisen when and because he has recognized the authoritative cosmic character of the challenge to which he has responded with a total all-embracing commitment. Now, he will say, is it conceivable that something so unique, final, all-compelling, as this can ever be associated with uncertainties of expression? Must not something as ultimate, satisfying, and far-reaching as this carry with it expressions of similar status?

Or perhaps the religious man's expectation of certainty has arisen in another way altogether—as a way of resolving a pastoral dilemma. For how can anybody proclaim a gospel—good news—if he is uncertain what to talk about? Must not a preacher be sure of his message?

[1] Butler's summary of the deist position, *Analogy*, pt. II. ch. VI. I.

B

How natural it is, then, nay it might seem as if it were essential, to claim to be sure in religion. Yet religious certainty has led to positions which not only unbelievers but many believers have found objectionable. The desire to be sure in religion leads, it will be said, to prejudice, bigotry and fanaticism. It leads to a dogmatism and to an authoritarianism that few would regard as virtues, for to compel without persuading is to compromise the very personalities which it is hoped to convince. Here is what John Locke aptly called an 'Egyptian bondage' with 'Egyptian darkness',[1] when 'parties of men' snuffed out the candle of the Lord which is the very spirit of man. Perhaps after all, we can be *too* sure in religion.

But—it might be said—that is not our difficulty today. The difficulty nowadays is to be sure enough. Our religious profession is challenged on every side. Pastorally we may talk of television, cheap excursions, the petrol engine, gardens, the wrong Archbishops, objections to envelope schemes, lack of heating in churches and chapels, bad timing of services, too much rain or too much sunshine at 10.50 on a Sunday morning—we may talk of all of these to account for the weakness of Christian witness. But may it not be partly at least because our contemporaries think we have nothing to say, or nothing to say which cannot be said better by somebody else? Let us frankly face it, we are in a most serious intellectual crisis that requires a major operation, which will test both the sympathetic sensitiveness of the surgeons and their intellectual skills and techniques, if we are to come out of it alive. Recall some of our perplexities. The critical, historical approach to the Bible makes any simple appeal to the Bible hazardous in the extreme: yet think only of the shock felt by many people when, presented with the New English Bible, they

[1] *Essay concerning Human Understanding*, Bk. IV. ch. 3. 20.

had their first uncertainties about the Lord's Prayer. At a more sophisticated level, the progress and accuracy of historical research make appeals to the past far more problematical than many arguments about (say) episcopacy or inter-communion suppose or suggest. Is it 'evident to all men',[1] diligence alone being required, that from the Apostles' time there have been Bishops, Priests and Deacons in Christ's Church? Again, it is a commonplace that contemporary politics and sociology raise far-reaching questions of the greatest significance for which there seem to be no specifically Christian answers. Developments in the natural sciences have brought with them a cosmology and a culture which we have still not sufficiently reckoned with. Developments in the biological sciences in particular threaten our most cherished concepts. Progress in molecular biology seems to some to erode the distinctive character of human life; the developments in neurology and psychiatry, especially the significance of cybernetics for the study of the brain, seem to play havoc with concepts such as responsibility, guilt and sin. Again, as the world shrinks, to make Indian temples as near as the television set, the comparative study of religions raises problems about the uniqueness and significance of the Christian faith. Finally even if philosophy no longer flourishes the nonsense veto which it did in the 'thirties, nevertheless it still presents us with a challenge—a challenge to religious people to elucidate the empirical anchorage of their religious assertions.

So the desire to be sure in religion, however natural, however understandable, however dangerous, seems in any case at the moment doomed to disappointment by an intellectual, practical, pastoral and evangelistic context of appalling complexity. Is religious certainty compatible

[1] Preface to the *Form and Manner of Making, Ordaining and Consecrating of Bishops, Priests and Deacons according to the Order of the Church of England.*

with an honest facing of the complexities which surround us?

It is at this point that F. D. Maurice becomes relevant and important. For F. D. Maurice can be seen as struggling to give some sort of answer to this very question—an 'obscure', 'misty and confused' answer perhaps[1]—in an age in which our present difficulties were a cloud no bigger than the size of a man's hand; and I believe that we may find in Maurice 'hints'[2] (one of his favourite words), hints towards a solution.

What I propose to do in this book is to take three themes characteristic of F. D. Maurice and to consider each in relation to this problem of being sure in religion. In the first chapter we shall have in mind the well-known controversy over eternal punishment; next, we shall consider the problem of certainty in Christian sociology; and thirdly we shall look at Maurice's views on subscription. In this first chapter, then, we shall consider eternal punishment.

Can we be sure about the doctrine of eternal punishment? And if and when we are, what are we sure of? To answer those questions let us first go back to Maurice. It is not hard to reconstruct the view of eternal punishment which he criticized in his day. It would begin with the Gospels and (say) the story of the sheep and the goats (Matt. xxv. 41). 'Then shall he say also unto them on the left hand: "Depart from me, ye cursed, into the eternal fire which is prepared for the devil and his angels, for I was an hungred, and ye gave me no meat . . ." ' Or in the N.E.B. ' "The curse is upon you; go from my sight to the eternal fire that is ready for the devil and his angels. For

---

[1] The words were used of Maurice by those who nevertheless acknowledged his greatness, C. F. G. Masterman and Benjamin Jowett respectively. See A. R. Vidler, *Witness to the Light*, pp. 4, 5.

[2] *loc. cit.* p. 16. Cp. footnote on 2 p. 17 below.

when I was hungry you gave me nothing to eat. . . ." '
Or if we have reservations over Matthew, there is Luke
and the parable of Dives and Lazarus (Luke xvi. 19–31).
'Abraham said, Son, remember that thou in thy life time
receivedst thy good things, and Lazarus in like manner
evil things; but now here he is comforted and thou art in
anguish.' Or, '. . . all the good things fell to you while you
were alive, and all the bad to Lazarus, now he has con-
solation here and it is you who are in agony' (N.E.B.).

Nothing was more natural than that these passages and
others like them should next lead directly to the theme of
sin—man in all his sinfulness. Such sinfulness (continues
the argument) God has a right to punish and in his
Judgment and Wrath *will* punish, unless we use the
Advocate provided as a propitiation for these sins—unless
we enter into the benefits of Christ's passion and accept
the gracious mercy of God which is now available since his
terrible justice has been satisfied in the crucifixion. The
alternative is punishment for ever in conditions so horrible
and inescapable as to terrify all except those destined to be
reprobate.

Here was a view sponsored by men who were undoubtedly sure of eternal punishment, who would argue
their case systematically, for whom everything was cut
and dried. Here and hereafter were understood as of one
piece. Of all such systems perhaps Calvinism was the most
comprehensive.[1]

What was Maurice's reaction to this doctrine? Let us
begin by reminding ourselves that Maurice was by our
standards very conservative. As Dr. Vidler reminds us,
any 'humane revulsion against the notion that the majority
of manhood could be doomed to eternal punishment' did

[1] Dr. Vidler (*loc. cit.* p. 52 n.) mentions that Maurice's mother and some
of his sisters were converted from Unitarianism to Calvinism.

not weigh much 'if at all, with Maurice'.[1] Further, though
Maurice 'was not afraid of Biblical criticism or of any
facts that science might disclose, he himself had no difficulty in accepting the historicity of the book of Genesis'.[2]
As he wrote elsewhere: 'The Fall is a fact of history, just
as the Bible presents it to us',[3] and he also accepted Archbishop Ussher's chronology. So there was nothing in
science or in biblical criticism, not even in morality, to
make Maurice less sure of the doctrine of eternal punishment than his opponents. Why then was he against it?

There seem to be two main reasons—the one negative,
the other positive.

1. What undoubtedly offended Maurice was the cut-
and-dried character of the doctrine, which possessed what
were for him all the objectionable signs of system. As
Dr. Vidler reminds us, Maurice displayed what has been
called 'system-phobia'.[4] Maurice says, for instance, in his
Moral and Metaphysical Philosophy, 'I have not aspired to
give an account of systems and schools . . . I take no
interest in the subject. I should have wearied myself and
my readers if I had endeavoured to pursue it.'[5] At the same
time, as Dr. Vidler points out, Maurice did not despise
logic or reasoning: 'It would be entirely to misunderstand
Maurice to suppose that, in attacking system-mongering,
he was opposing order, logic and method in theology.'[6]
System he might abhor, but reasonable discourse he
valued and sought after. 'To me', he said, 'these words

[1] *loc. cit.* p. 34.
[2] *loc. cit.* p. 34.
[3] *Doctrine of Sacrifice*, p. 287, quoted by Dr. Vidler, *loc. cit.* p. 34, footnote 1.
[4] Quoted by Dr. Vidler, *loc. cit.* p. 9, from *The Life of Frederick Denison Maurice*, edited by his son (1884 ed.), ii. 43.
[5] Quoted by Dr. Vidler, *loc. cit.* p. 13, from *Moral and Metaphysical Philosophy*, II. vii.
[6] Dr. Vidler, *loc. cit.* p. 12.

(*system* and *method*) seem not only not synonymous, but the greatest contraries imaginable: the one indicating that which is most opposed to life, freedom and variety: and the other that without which they cannot exist.'[1] Indeed, with what we might think is a curious anticipation of the interests of contemporary philosophy, Maurice is convinced of the usefulness of concerning ourselves with language: 'The cure for the extreme lust of distinction is certainly not found in overlooking distinctions or denying their importance. It is not found by shrinking from the severe examination of words and of their shades of meaning. The more carefully that examination is pursued, the more we are led to feel the significance and sacredness of words, the less we are likely to play dishonest tricks with them. That words are things, mighty and terrible things, was the special lesson which the middle ages had to learn, and which they had to impart.'[2] So the liberal Dean Church could remark of Maurice that he had a lesson of immense importance to teach us—that we must 'look into the meaning of our familiar words, and try to use them with a real meaning'.[3] It is a slogan which the contemporary empiricist repeats in a new setting, and against a new background.

2. Where, however, would this 'real meaning' be found? —which leads us to Maurice's second and more positive answer. This is that the 'real meaning' of all theological phrases is to be found in God—that we have understood no Bible story, understood no doctrine, professed no Creed, used no prayer book in worship unless we have

---

[1] Quoted by Dr. Vidler, *loc. cit.* p. 13, from *The Kingdom of Christ* (Ev. ed.), I. 238.

[2] Quoted by Dr. Vidler, *loc. cit.* p. 12, from *Moral and Metaphysical Philosophy*, I. 577.

[3] Quoted by Dr. Vidler, *loc. cit.* p. 13, from R. W. Church, *Occasional Papers* (1897), II. 309 f.

thereby found and known God. This seems to me to be Maurice's penetrating insight, his major claim, and one with immense significance for our own day.

How in particular did Maurice work this out in the matter of eternal punishment? Suppose we look at his *Theological Essays*.

Even those who have most successfully preached the doctrine, those who have thereby stirred their hearers to belief, have succeeded (Maurice would say) because they preached better than they knew.

Think of any sermon of a Methodist preacher which roused the heart of a Kingswood collier, or of a dry, hard, formal man, or of a contented, self-righteous boaster of his religion, in the last century. You will say he talked of an infinite punishment which God might inflict on them all if they continued disobedient. He may have talked of that, but he would have talked till doomsday if he had not spoken another language too, which interpreted this, and into which the conscience rapidly translated it. He spoke of an infinite *Sin*: he spoke of an infinite *Love*: he spoke of that which was true then, whatever might be true hereafter. He said 'Thou art in a wrong state: hell is about thee. God would bring thee into a right state: He would save thee out of that hell.' The man believed the words; something within him told him they were true. I cannot tell what vanities and confusions might come to him afterwards, from his own dreams or the crudities of his teachers. But I am sure this was not a delusion—could not be. He *had* escaped from the twilight: he *had* seen the opposite forms of light and darkness no longer miserably confused together. Good was all good; evil was all evil: there was war in heaven and earth between them; in him, even in him, where the battle had been fiercest, the odds against the good greatest, it had gotten the victory. He had a right to believe that the morning stars were singing together at the news of it; otherwise, why was there such music in his, the Kingswood collier's, heart?

If such processes are rare in our days, it is, I believe, because the descendants of these Methodist preachers, and we in imitation of them, fancy that the mere machinery, whether earthly or divine, which they put in motion, was the cause of them,— because we do not thoroughly understand or heartily believe that there is that war of Life and Death, of Good and Evil, now in every man's heart, as there was of old. Therefore, we do not speak straightly and directly to both. We suppose men are to be shown by arguments that they have sinned, and that God has a right to punish them. We do not say to them, 'You are under a law of love; you know you are, and you are fighting with it.'[1]

The reference to Methodist preaching may or may not have been historically and psychologically true, but I am quite sure that Maurice's account of the *logic* of the matter is reliable enough.[2] The principal theme, the 'real meaning' of 'eternal punishment', is known when and only when the phrase somehow leads us to realize 'the infinite love of God'.[3]

The same conclusion is to be found when he considers Eternal Death at the end of his *Theological Essays*. Here was a question (he says) 'proved by a thousand indications to be especially occupying this age',[4] and it is interesting to find that when allowance is made for some dated terminology, Maurice's account of the situation is not without

[1] *Theological Essays*, ed. E. F. Carpenter (1957), pp. 35–6.
[2] Cp. 'Fanaticism and even consciously dishonest quackery cannot produce any results unless they have some true principle to work with.' Quoted Vidler, *loc. cit.* p. 11, from *The Kingdom of Christ*, I. 145 (Ev. ed.).
[3] Cp. Maurice's Preface in the second edition of the *Theological Essays* (1853). 'I plead for the Love of God, . . . not for a mercy which relaxes the penalties of it' (xxii). 'I call upon them to join us in acknowledging God's love and his redemption first of all, and then to consider earnestly what is or what is not compatible with that acknowledgment' (xxiii). 'I hold the Bible to be the Book of Life; I see it turned into a Book of Death' (xxiv).
[4] *Theological Essays* (1853 second edition), p. 432.

its echoes today. 'I have spoken of Eternal *Life*; what is
Eternal *Death*? Dare we think of it?' Or alternatively,

Must we not try [he says] in some way, to evade the consideration of it—to explain away the words of Scripture, which
suggest it to us?

Unitarians have tried to explain them away. A number of
the most wise, devout, excellent men living now, or that have
lived, in our own Church, and among the Dissenters, have
shrunk from them. We have the testimony of persons very com-
petent to speak, from the extent and variety of their experience,
whose veracity is unquestionable, that multitudes of the upper
classes are scared into infidelity by them. They furnish, as
many clergymen in metropolitan parishes know, some of the
most plausible and effective arguments against Christianity,
to those who lecture among the lower classes. Again and again,
one finds earnest and devout persons asking how they can
reconcile them with that Gospel of God's Love, which they
must hold fast, whatever else they part with.

The trouble is (Maurice believes) that

divines, even good and earnest men, were anxious to get a
much *more* formal and distinct assertion of the doctrine of
Everlasting Punishment than the older Confessions supply.
Our Reformers having introduced an Article upon it into the
Forty-two which were originally drawn up for the use of the
English Church, omitted that Article in the Thirty-nine. For
some reason or other, they judged it more right and more safe,
even in so complete a compendium as that—intended for the
student and the guide of others—not to put forth a dogmatic
statement on this subject.[1]

But others have found it much harder to shrink from dogmatism, much easier in that way to be sure in religion.

Now comes Maurice's most considered expression of his
views on eternal punishment. His answer is that we fix on

[1] *Theological Essays* (1853), pp. 432-3.

the word 'eternal', and whether the original of Matt. xxv was in Aramaic or Syriac or Greek, seek to discover (he says) 'the inner life of the words'—that which is 'forgotten in the customary use of them'.[1]

The word 'eternal' is a keyword of the New Testament. To draw our minds from the temporal, to fix them on the eternal, is the very aim of the divine economy. How much ought we then, to dread any confusion between thoughts which our Lord has taken such pains to keep distinct,—which our conscience tell us ought to be kept distinct! How dangerous to introduce the notion of duration into a word from which He has deliberately excluded it! And yet this is precisely what we are in the habit of doing, and it is this which causes such infinite perplexity to our minds. 'Try to conceive', the teacher says, 'a thousand years. Multiply these by a thousand, by twenty thousand, by a hundred thousand, by a million. Still you are as far off from eternity as ever.' Certainly I am, quite as far. Why then did you give me that sum to work out? What could be the use of it, except to bewilder me, except to make me disbelieve in Eternity altogether? Do you not see that this course must be utterly wrong and mischievous? If Eternity is the great reality of all, and not a portentous fiction, how dare you impress such a notion of fictitiousness on my mind as your process of illustration conveys? 'But is it not the only process?' —Quite the only one, so far as I see, if you will bring Time into the question; if you will have years, and centuries, to prevent you from taking in the sublime truth, 'This is life eternal, to know God.'[2]

In short, we must so talk about eternity, even Eternal Punishment or Eternal Death, that the phrases lead to God. The righteous (Matt. xxv) go to eternal life, yes: but that is a phrase to be taken (says Maurice) in the context of John xvii. 3: 'This is Life Eternal, that they may know Thee, the only true God, and Jesus Christ whom

[1] *loc. cit.* p. 435.   [2] *loc. cit.* p. 436.

Thou hast sent.'[1] As for eternal punishment—'this is the loss of that power of perceiving His love, [it is to have] the incapacity of loving: no greater damnation can befall any. And yet, as long as that word "punishment" is used—as long as it is represented as the act of a Father—the heart discovers—cannot help discovering—a hope even in his deprivation.'[2]

So Maurice pegs back the doctrine into the love of God:

Christ's Gospel reveals an abyss of love . . . I am content to be lost in that. I know no more, but I am sure that there is a woe on us if we do not preach this Gospel, if we do not proclaim the name of the Father, the Son and the Spirit—the Eternal Charity. Whenever we do proclaim that Name, I believe we invade the realm of Night and Eternal Death, and open the Kingdom of Heaven.[3]

For (as he has said earlier),

What is Death Eternal, but to be without God? What is that infinite dread which rises upon my mind, which I cannot banish from me, when I think of my own godlessness and lovelessness,—that I may become wholly separated from Love; become wholly immersed in selfishness and hatred? What dread can I have—ought I to have—besides this? What other can equal this? Mix up with this, the consideration of days and years and millenniums, you add nothing either to my comfort or my fears. All you do is to withdraw me from the real cause of my misery, which is my separation from the source of life and peace; from the hope which must come to me in one place or another, if I can again believe in God's love and cast myself upon it.[4]

Before discussing Maurice's position, there are two other points that are worthy of note:

1. What on this account do we make of purgatory?

[1] Quoted *loc. cit.* p. 437.   [2] *loc. cit.* p. 438.
[3] *loc. cit.* pp. 442–3.   [4] *loc. cit.* p. 437.

It cannot be denied [says Maurice] that men are escaping to Rome in search of a purgatory, because they see in that, some token that God is merciful to his creatures, that the whole mass of human beings in our streets and alleys whom we have overlooked and neglected, nineteen hundredths of the population of all the Continental countries, most of the American Slaves, besides the whole body of Turks, Hindoos, Hottentots, Jews, will not sink for ever, in a short time, into hopeless destruction, from which a few persons, some of whom are living comfortably, eating their dinners and riding in their carriages without any vexation of heart, may by special mercy, be delivered. They say this is the meaning of what they have been told in the land where a Gospel is said to be preached, where Bibles are distributed in every village. They say that a Church which gives them a hope that this is not so, that the threescore years and ten do not absolutely limit the compassion of the Father of Spirits, must be better than the one in which they have been bred.[1]

The worry is that the Reformers' criticisms of Purgatory are still (for Maurice) well-founded—the over-confident, over-systematic developments, the 'idle fancies about places where spirits may be dwelling', 'the blasphemous notion of paying so much to God for bringing souls out of the condition which belongs to them'[2] and so on. . . . But in losing the doctrine of Purgatory we have lost (acknowledges Maurice) some insight into God's love and charity, and such insight Maurice would fain preserve. Not that Maurice is a universalist: this too would be systematizing —being over-sure about our religion.

2. The second point worthy of special note concerns the Athanasian Creed. What of the Athanasian Creed?

If the Creed had meant that the not holding certain intellectual notions concerning the Trinity involved the penalty of everlasting death, it would consign to destruction, not [only]

[1] *loc. cit.* pp. 439–40.   [2] *loc. cit.* p. 441.

heretics,—extreme or moderate—but every peasant, every child, nearly every woman in every congregation in which it is read, seeing that these (thank God) have formed no such intellectual conceptions, that the majority are not capable of forming them. And the few persons it would count worthy of eternal life, are a set of schoolmen, the best of whom pray every day and hour, that they may become as little children, and have the faith which those have, who do not look upon the subject from a logical point of view at all. Lastly, it would directly contradict its own most solemn assertions. If we could comprehend this truth in an intellectual statement, the Father would *not* be incomprehensible, the Son incomprehensible, the Holy Ghost incomprehensible. But since there is no alternative between this utterly monstrous imagination, and that which supposes the Creed to affirm the knowledge of God and eternal life to be the same; and therefore the denial,—not in the letter, but in the spirit,—not intellectual and outwardly, but morally and inwardly—of the Father, Son and Spirit, to be eternal death,—I cannot help thinking that, with all its fierce language, it has a gentler heart than some of those who get themselves credit for Toleration, by wishing the Church well rid of it. *They* leave us free to judge occasionally, to assume a portion of God's authority, only protesting against any excessive intrusion into it. The Creed obliges us to give such a meaning to eternal life—or rather to adhere so closely to our Lord's explanation of it—that we have no power of saying, in any case, who has lost it, or incurred the state which is opposite to it.[1]

Maurice well recognizes that people will challenge him with the question: but is this what the writer meant? And Maurice's answer deserves our closest attention, for the question is, as we shall see presently, apt to be put to anyone who recommends a new logical allocation of traditional phrases.[2]

If I am asked [says Maurice, continuing the discussion] whether the writer did not suppose that he had this power, I answer;

[1] *loc. cit.* pp. 445–6.   [2] See below, p. 20.

'When you tell me who the writer was, I may possibly, though probably not even then, be able to make some guess whether he supposed it or not. At present, I am quite in the dark about him and his motives. If I adopt the theory, which is as reasonable as any other, that he lived in the time of the Vandal persecution, I think it is very likely that along with a much deepened conviction of the worth of the principle for which he was suffering, he had also a mixture of earthly passion and fierceness, and that he was tempted to show his opponents, or those who were apostatising, that there were more terrible penalties than those of scourging the back or cutting out the tongue. In that case, I should say I *was* giving up that part of his *animus* which he would wish me to give up; that part which was not of God, and could not be meant to abide; and was clinging to that which made his other words true and consistent with themselves, when I interpreted his Creed in conformity with our Lord's sentence. I should not be imitating the treatment which Mr. Ward (in his Ideal of the Church) applied to our Articles, (I have no doubt he is one of those on whom Romanism has conferred a benefit by making him at least respectful of the formularies by which he is bound), when he maintained that a non-natural sense might be put on them because the compilers of them meant to cheat Catholics, and Catholics might pay them in their own coin. I should apply just the opposite rule. If I found a general scope of meaning which was important and precious, and which belonged to all times, I should not sacrifice that for the sake of a portion which belonged to the circumstances and feelings of a particular time or a particular man. To use Mr. Canning's celebrated simile, I should not follow the example of those worshippers of the Sun, who chose the moment of an eclipse to come forth with their hymns and their symbols.[1]

So to our own day. As I see it, we have three major lessons to learn from Maurice as we try to elucidate theological certainty:

[1] *loc. cit.* pp. 446–7.

(i) The need to peg back all our assertions into an awareness of God.

(ii) The need to be circumspect of any too extensive systematization, of any cut-and-dried theology.

(iii) The recognition that lack of such logical circumspection can lead to blunders which darken the light of God.

With these reflections in mind, how do we best understand eternal punishment? Maurice, I suggest, was undoubtedly right in remarking at the outset that 'eternal' is *not* synonymous with 'everlasting', if 'everlasting' is taken to mean 'going on in a continuous time-series for ever and ever', and he is also right when he suggests, apropos Matt. xxv. 46, and in criticism of the Authorized Version,[1] that we cannot consistently translate αἰώνιος 'eternal' when it qualifies life, and yet 'everlasting' when it qualifies punishment. In both cases 'eternal' is logically odd, though we normally have a hunch of this only with the second case; and in both cases we may well bring to our aid to get a line on this oddness, the Platonic context in which Maurice generally set his words (not least because he discerned no system in Plato).[2] Undoubtedly the point of the word 'eternal' is 'to draw our minds from the temporal, to fix them' elsewhere. But while we shall certainly be muddled if we see both an antithesis *and* a parallel between eternal and temporal, while we shall certainly blunder if after distinguishing the eternal from the temporal we merely take it to be 'unending time', Maurice I suggest is perhaps a little too nervous of the time reference. Why not see the word 'eternal' as one which, *beginning* with a temporal

---

[1] By now Maurice would have the support of the Revisers, R.V., R.S.V., and N.E.B.

[2] In his attitude to Plato, he might well find support today from Professor A. H. Armstrong.

reference, will help to 'draw our minds' from *fixing* on it? When we take a span of a thousand years, multiply it by one thousand, twenty thousand, one hundred thousand, a million, and so on, admittedly we are at every stage 'as far off from eternity as ever'.[1] But that is the very point of the exercise: there *is* no *end* to the story: and we continue it not because at some point 'eternal' will measure the time-span we have then covered, but precisely because at some point or other we hope by this means to evoke a disclosure—when the phrase will have been used—as Maurice wished—*to bring us to God*.[2]

Let me develop this suggestion by considering the phrase 'eternal punishment' in rather more detail. We can best construe this kind of phrase as what I have called else-where a qualified model.[3] Why do I speak of 'model'? Well, models are of use when they are acceptable, per-suasive, clear and so reliable guides to what at the present

---

[1] Similarly with an infinite sequence in mathematics, e.g. $\frac{1}{2}$, $\frac{2}{3}$, $\frac{3}{4}$, $\frac{4}{5}$, $\frac{5}{6}$, $\frac{6}{7}$, $\frac{7}{8}$ ... $\frac{999}{1000}$ ... we may be said at any stage to be 'as far off' unity 'as ever'. But it is equally true that while there is no end to the story so that we may continue it as far as we like, nevertheless at some stage or other—sooner or later—we may 'see' that to which the sequence is 'pointing', viz. 1.

[2] Cp. what Maurice says about a disclosure of eternity in the course of a discussion on the Trinity: 'The more we attend to the New Testament, the more we find to confirm the witness of our reason, that eternity is not a lengthening out or continuation of time: that they are generically differ-ent. ... If you have listened with earnestness to the questions of a child, you may often think that it knows more of eternity than of time. The succession of years confounds it: it mixes the dates which it has been instructed in most strangely; but its intuition of something which is beyond all dates makes you marvel. ... With these hints, which every day's reading of the Scriptures ... will multiply and expand, what need we have of some direct words to bring together the two thoughts of Eternity and of Life.' *Theological Essays*, ed. E. F. Carpenter (1957), p. 294. Here are 'hints' towards an 'intuition' of what is 'beyond all dates' though it may have been generated by a temporal series.

[3] See e.g. *Religious Language* ch. II, and *Freedom and Immortality* especially pp. 92–100.

C

baffles us. So I use the word 'model' of the word which all of us would take 'as read'. Now with Maurice we will undoubtedly see puzzles circulating round the word 'eternal': not so around 'punishment'. All of us who have bent before schoolmasters, or prostrated ourselves before pink-ticket policemen, or stood before an array of magistrates, have a clear idea of punishment. Here are clear pictures of opposition and antithesis.

The situation, however, may be too plain—so plain as to lack any moral features. The Clerk to the Justices may know their Worships' prejudices; the pink tickets may be regarded as only part of an outdoor parlour game to encourage young policemen when greater captures elude them; the schoolmaster may be merely working off chronic indigestion. But if punishment is to be a suitable model for use in religious discourse, it must certainly express some kind of *moral discernment*. We must talk of how such and such an act of brutal murder or rape deserves punishment —carries with it categorically some kind of moral offensiveness to which we *must* match some appropriate moral response—indeed the whole practical difficulty of punishment is to devise reputable ways and means of expressing this moral response which do not by their very execution create more moral offence than the occasion which called them forth.

'Punishment' in this way must always fit into a recognizable moral context of separation, opposition, antithesis. But the schoolmaster's joviality returns. To the parent he praises a 'delightfully mischievous' son. We go to the police ball and join in the happy fraternity. Nay more, even punishment in the most serious of moral contexts comes to an end: all human punishment is in that sense of finite duration. Hence the point of the qualifier 'eternal'. The point of the qualifier is to remove from punishment stories any restriction whatever of space and time, until there is disclosed to us the condition of those who are apart from God, and on the subjective side it is appropriately characterized by Maurice as infinite dread'[1]—another qualified model.

But the story does not conclude at that point. The Christian will claim that the very moment of disclosure, when we contemplate indeed the depths of 'eternal punishment', may also be the occasion of *finding* God. How? Well, reflect that those for whom the moment of greatest antagonism calls forth the greatest sympathy, are said to display 'redeeming love'. . . . Hence, the preaching of Eternal Punishment may in fact be a way of leading men to a vision of God's infinite love. Here is the essential part of the doctrine. But as Maurice recognizes, the model we develop must not be that of Headmaster or Policeman or Magistrate, or even that impressive epitome of Justice, the Assize Court Judge. The model (as we have just hinted) must be that of a loving Father who, in loving, redeems. When the loving father punishes (in whatever way he judges best) the sense of opposition and separation which undoubtedly occurs, nevertheless yields at its climax a kinship of deeper love—a richer reconciliation. It is in terms of this model—as qualified and developed— that eternal punishment is to be understood.

In ways like this, then, in terms of contemporary empirical insights, we may elucidate Maurice's attempt to ground all these phrases in God, even in God and his Love. We may emphasize with Maurice that eternal punishment talks of God, not of a cosmic extension of our penal system. But the contemporary approach has perhaps the merit of making a distinction which Maurice did not discern. Maurice, it will be recalled, takes 'Eternal

[1] See above, on p. 12, quotation from Maurice, *loc. cit.* p. 437.

Punishment' and 'Eternal Death' as synonyms. But our approach enables us to make a distinction here. For it is clear that 'Eternal Death' works in terms of another model 'death'—the cessation of all our overt behaviour. So 'eternal death' is a phrase by means of which we may approach the concept of utter annihilation, which is another situation in which God's infinite love is disclosed, as human love can best be disclosed to men who feel utterly isolated, forsaken, alone.

Now at this point it might be objected to me as to Maurice:[1] does such a treatment of these phrases do justice to what Christians have often said and talked of and preached? What have we to say about that? Undoubtedly some Christians *have* taken theological language at its face value and have had no inhibitions about expanding it *ad lib.*[2] They have supposed that people like Milton and Dante have produced the colour slides (so to say) of a future world tour. Lurid pictures have been drawn of the Great Assize and the Great Reckoning. But if they have been no more than those words suggest, how far have they been religious pictures? I do not want to deny that faith may have discerned, even in the crudest pictures, what Maurice calls the 'inner meanings' of the words: but all of us recognize that countless people have *not* so discerned. The Great Assize is then as much the occasion of ribald mirth as of religious devotion. We recall the old story of the Master of Trinity, Cambridge, rising with customary *largesse* when proceedings had terminated on the Day of Judgment. He rose (he said) to propose a vote of thanks to one who (he need hardly remind the company) was the

[1] Professor Lewis rightly put this question to me in an article in the *Hibbert Journal*, January 1961; and see above, p. 14.

[2] Though like Maurice with the Athanasian Creed we may always distinguish between the admittedly ephemeral and the permanent features of Christian arguments.

oldest Trinity man, and who had presided with such distinction on what had been for everybody concerned a rather trying occasion. Here is religious language so misunderstood as to be a common-room joke. Let us acknowledge in frank honesty that Christians have mis-read the logic of the phrase 'eternal punishment', not least theologians who have so often built out arguments from the most prosaic features of the pictures. But a greater caution is abroad today. Even Reinhold Niebuhr, who could not be accused of a watery liberalism, warns us: 'It is unwise for Christians to claim any knowledge of either the furniture of heaven or the temperature of hell: or to be too certain about any details of the Kingdom of God.'[1] And if anyone is overwhelmed with a sense of loss at being deprived of details of heaven and hell, let him at least not forget the immense gain which also comes from these logical insights. Eternal punishment might conflict —certainly will conflict—with infinite love when both phrases are wrongly allocated. Eternal Punishment will lead to insuperable difficulties when it is wrongly struc-tured—when the wrong model is taken or inadequately qualified. It is not the least merit of Maurice that he gives us a 'hint' as to how the conflict can logically, though never 'systematically', be overcome.

We have now come full circle; and we may ask again: what has become of Christian certainty? Of what are we sure in the doctrine of eternal punishment if we are *not* to be sure of the temperature of hell, nor to cherish that picture of the Grand Assize or the brimstone lake? Of *what* are we sure? What is left? I answer, all that matters—*God*. But, you will say (and I recognize this to be behind Pro-fessor Lewis's objections) can no more be said?

The answer is that it can—but never without logical

[1] *The Nature and Destiny of Man.* Vol. II, *Human Destiny*, ch. x, p. 304.

circumspection. For once we are logically cautious, once we accept the logical restrictions built into the qualifier, we may readily recognize the propriety and usefulness of translating the phrase 'eternal punishment' into countless pictures—verbal and non-verbal models—which then allow for its readier assimilation, which allow for that talking which, with Augustine,[1] we may thus regard as an unfortunate necessity because always inadequate while inevitable. We may speak picturesquely of 'God's punishment' in terms of a Great Assize, a division of sheep and goats, a great gulf between heaven and hell—models indeed. We may also speak of 'God's punishment' along the lines suggested by, and with the kind of justification made by Joseph Butler: 'A moral scheme of governments . . . [being] visibly established' in the natural world, 'this together with the essential tendencies of virtue and vice . . . naturally raise in us an apprehension that it will be carried on further towards perfection in a future state and that everyone shall there receive according to his deserts'. So there is 'in the very nature of the thing a tendency to their being rewarded and punished'.[2] Here is a rather more sophisticated model-language—the language of morals. Possibilities of modelling are endless: but so are the problems. Cosmology will play a stop card somewhere as we develop our picture of the Grand Assize; even morality will bring its own self-criticisms: can any behaviour be

---

[1] Cp. *De Trinitate*: 'Tamen cum quaeritur quid tres, magna prorsus inopia humanum laborat eloquium. Dictum est tamen tres personae, non ut illud diceretur, sed ne taceretur' (V. 10). ('When the question is asked —what three?—human language labours under an altogether great poverty of speech. The answer, however, is given—three persons—not that it might be adequately talked about, but to avoid silence.') Cp. what he says in VII. 9 about human weakness endeavouring 'to utter in speech to the senses of man what it grasps in the secret places of the mind'.

[2] *The Analogy*, Concl. I. 132.

evil enough to deserve (morally) a punishment that never ceases? In all these ways we shall be warned against system-building—we shall be warned against spreading ourselves in too wide a field of inferences. Let no one deny the need and usefulness of what we may call theological approximation to—picturesque projections of—doctrine. There is nothing disreputable about them *provided that* we recognize them for the approximations they are. Further, if there is one principle to be borne in mind when making a comparative assessment of theological approximations, it is: the *more* we say, the more we need to be cautious about *what* we say. So what Maurice suggests—and what I too suggest—is that we can be sure of God, yet tentative about our theology. Let us frankly acknowledge theological uncertainties. Let us not conceal them from our congregations or our audiences; let us not perpetuate schemes that demand or imply greater certainty than we possess. Still more, let us not build, on mistaken foundations, vast systems which suffocate religion. Let us acknowledge where at various points we are doctrinally 'unsure' . . . recognizing that it is *not* inconsistent to claim at the same time that we are sure of God—God given to us in a disclosure to which all our language can at best only lead, and which all our discursive theology will ever inadequately try to talk about, of which all our pictures are at best temporal projections. These are themes to which I will return in the chapters that follow.

Meanwhile, may I give a well-worn example to suggest that this union of religious certainty with theological approximation—being sure in religion but tentative in theology—is not an unreasonable position? I am *not* claiming logical identity between mathematics and theology, I am not denying that the illustration implies all sorts of background difficulties. But I give it for what it is worth.

Consider a series of circles and their diameters:

There is a sense in which this series (continued *ad infinitum*) might lead to a disclosure of π. We may 'see' by means of this sequence that the circumferences divided by the diameters gives an invaraint. If so, we will be *sure* of π. But when we try to express this π in language which everyone will receive, we never reach beyond uncertainty—we have what might be called 'numerical uncertainty'. First, there is the familiar $\frac{22}{7}$, then $3 \cdot 142$; better: $3 \cdot 14159$. Or, to show that there is room for untold diversity, recall that another approximation to π is given by counting the letters in successive words of the sentence: 'Can I remember the reciprocal?' and dividing the result, i.e. $\cdot 318310$ into 1, and so on. More sophisticatedly, π is $4(1 - \frac{1}{3} + \frac{1}{5} - \frac{1}{7} + \frac{1}{9} \ldots)$, and the story is again unending, but progressively more accurate. Does anyone think badly of numerical approximation? Not at all. Many engineers thrive on $\frac{22}{7}$, but they must always carry at the back of their minds the necessary corrective—remembering that it is in fact only an approximation. We may be sure of π when the diagrams disclose it, but we are always numerically approximate in our understanding of it. In something like the same way, in being sure of eternal punishment we are sure only of God: all other models are approximate—more or less.

As is well known, it was because of his views on eternal

punishment, and especially as these were expressed in his *Theological Essays* from which I quoted earlier with such sympathy, that F. D. Maurice left King's College in 1853. This was the book which provoked the crisis resulting in his resignation. Now it was in 1854 that F. D. Maurice, having left King's, started his Working Men's College to forward his social convictions. So it accords with biographical fact as well as with my own plans, that in the next chapter we shall turn to sociology. Can we be sure about our Christian social duty?

II

CHRISTIAN SOCIAL DUTY

WE started the book by enumerating some of the questions which our topic provokes. Can we not expect to be sure in a matter of such importance as religion? Surely God will guarantee his own revelation? Yet (we reflected) have not some believers been *too* sure in religion—displaying prejudice, bigotry and fanaticism? But (we hastened to add) the trouble today is rather that it is difficult to be sure at all. We then tried to get to grips with some of the basic issues needing to be settled before these questions are answered, by considering the celebrated phrase 'eternal punishment' which played such a significant part in the controversy which surrounded F. D. Maurice, and led to his departure from King's College. Maurice, we acknowledged, was right in criticizing those who fixed the phrase 'eternal punishment' squarely within a temporal context, who thus developed systematically the most confident assertions about a heaven and a hell. Here was theological certainty suffocating religion in a cast-iron grip—with God, at best, a superior Assize Judge or, at worst, a namesake of the Master of Trinity. It was Maurice's merit to discover that we could be sure in religion without claiming such theological certainty as this, without implying such theological absurdities, and what I tried to do in speaking of qualified models, and in giving the illustration of π, was to suggest that contemporary insights into the character of religious language and its empirical anchorage can perhaps do something to illuminate and explicate both Maurice's own positive contentions, and the criticisms he

made of his opponents. Our broad conclusion was that
Maurice's opponents were theologically so certain as to be
(on that account) questionably religious. But fortunately,
we said, there is an alternative: to be sure in religion but
tentative in theology, to unite religious certainty with
theological approximation . . . a need which is much less
revolutionary and altogether more acceptable today than
in Maurice's time—Maurice himself having contributed
not a little to this change of heart and mind, to what is
indeed a broader concept of reasonableness.

Now it is one of the curious ironies of the religious life
that what has been thought by very many to be a vice in
belief, has been hailed as a virtue in behaviour. Believers
and unbelievers who have assailed dogmatism and authoritarianism in belief, have quite often united again to
deplore the fact that the Christian faith gives no clear,
unambiguous answers on current social issues. The most
liberally-minded in theology have often sponsored the
greatest dogmatism over Christian social pronouncements. On the other hand, as I remarked in my last chapter, it might be said that today, far from our being too
sure or too confident about theology and social pronouncements, there is a malaise lying over both. Can we be sure
of our Christian social duty? Or: in being sure of our
Christian social duty, what are we being sure of? Notice
how the same question recurs, directed only to a different
topic. Can we be sure about eternal punishment, about
our Christian duty, and so on? Or: *in being sure* about
eternal punishment, about our Christian duty and so on,
what are we being sure of?

Let me make it clear at the outset that apart from a few
reflections at one point, I am not concerned in this chapter
to formulate or to discuss specific social pronouncements:
my task is once again what Locke would have called

under-labouring.[1] My interest is in a topic which lies behind all Christian social pronouncements, which all such pronouncements presuppose. My interest is in the question: what sort of certainty can we at best expect to reach, at what sort of certainty may we aim, in a Christian sociology?

There is hardly a Church Assembly passes, hardly a Church newspaper is published, without someone asking for a Christian sociology, a Christian social theory, a Christian social policy, a Christian strategy, asking that Christian doctrine be related to the social order, asking for a theology of society. What in fact is being asked for?

One way of recognizing the ambiguity of the demand is to look at the word 'policy'. On the one hand it may mean as the *Oxford English Dictionary* tells us: political sagacity, insight, state-craft . . . odd words whose reference is decidedly elusive. But these shade into something quite different: particular courses of action, generalizations implied by such actions, a particular formulation of principles, some kind of political system. Here we have our old antithesis again: Maurice's antithesis between insight and system—or, if we may so express it, between intuitive conviction and systematic certainty.

Now this ambiguity in the word 'policy' is reflected in two very different concepts of 'Christian social policy' which I propose now to examine in turn. The one talks in terms of a practical application of theological doctrines, in terms of a set of pronouncements, which could give the Church's unambiguous judgments on social problems, from capital punishment to contraception, from Sunday beer in Llandaff to daily bingo in Brighton. The other talks in terms of a Christian social policy where an endeavour is made to match social problems with Christian

---

[1] *Essay concerning Human Understanding*. Epistle to the Reader, p. 7 (A. S. Pringle-Pattison's abridged edition).

insights, whose translation thereafter into precepts and behaviour will inevitably be problematical. The two versions represent the tension in F. D. Maurice between a theological system and that God-discernment which (as he says in a pamphlet on subscription[1] which we shall consider in the next chapter) 'words may speak of but cannot embody.' Let us look then at each concept in turn, and we will call them respectively the linear-systematic, and the empirical-exploratory.

With the first approach, the method is to fix on certain doctrines, or texts, and to argue deductively from them so as to reach conclusions which elucidate current social issues, and solve current social problems. We fix on what would be called 'appropriate doctrines', and from these doctrines develop some generalization that is then applied to a particular social problem. Let us take a few examples.

Start with the doctrine of original sin. Suppose this is taken at least to assert, in the customary metaphors, that human nature is permanently infected, that all our decisions are entangled in a net of corruption and so on . . . well, one possible resultant generalization could be 'Whatever you do makes things worse.' The outcome could be a neutral pessimistic attitude to the world—believing that while it cannot be much improved, we might do at least a little (but not over much) to tidy up the necessary evil. Make do and hardly mend. Men will hardly do without prostitution—but at least let us keep the pavements clear.

Others of a different hue would start with doctrines of Creation and Natural Law, and see here the basis for such claims as are made respectively for the equality of man (in that garden of Eden, 'when Adam delved and Eve

[1] *Thoughts on the Rule of Conscientious Subscription* . . ., p. 13.

span, who was then a gentleman?'[1]—so: a plague on social classes) and the dependence of morality on God (so: 'the cure for delinquency is to make children go to Sunday School'). But neither of these examples of course comes anywhere near to the systematic comprehensiveness of Calvin's theocratic system with its claim to elucidate a civic and social pattern which was Christian through and through, from its doctrine of God and his grace to Ordinances which governed the Church, through a 'consistory' which was a tribunal of morals, to a prohibition of dancing and games.

Along with these, and as a final specimen of this first type of Christian social theory, we might perhaps mention Hegel, whose philosophy was thought at least by some to express the eternal truths of the gospel which were then, by courtesy of the Hegelian dialectic, given their civic and national implications. Here was Hegel providing a sort of translation service for Christian social action.

Now there are two general criticisms of this type of approach, and they centre around its beginning and end respectively:

1. *From where and on what grounds do we derive our starting point?*

Here there are at least two problems not necessarily disconnected; one, the collection of 'appropriate doctrines', and the other the adequate understanding of these doctrines or texts.

When it comes to formulating 'appropriate doctrines' Christians have undoubtedly tended to be self-restricting, and to talk in terms of single-key words—so that the whole of Christian theology has often been considered to spread with systematic neatness from one particular theme, e.g.

[1] To quote the text of John Ball's revolutionary sermon preached at Blackheath on the outbreak of the Peasants' Revolt, 1381.

'Justification by faith' or 'The Word of God' or '*Sola Gratia*'.

But such fragmentation,[1] whether biblical or doctrinal, while it leads to the easier and neater development of a system, does no justice to the complexity of the Christian faith, and inevitably leads to one-sided social because one-sided theological judgments. It is by now a well-known, not to say commonplace, criticism of Hegel that his system compromises rather than expresses distinctive Christian insights. In this Hegel is typical; to select single doctrines may make for neatness, but it is certainly theologically, and in this case also morally, compromising.

2. As a second criticism of this type of approach we may point out that *the linear derivation of social generalizations from theological assertions is hazardous in the extreme*, not least because the connection is most easily made by a sheer ignoring of the logical peculiarity of theological language. It is true that all social generalizations will, for the Christian, *presuppose* God: but that is not to say that they can be *deduced from* theological assertions. To suppose so is to confuse presuppositions and axioms.

We need not be surprised, then, to find diversity unlimited when, on this first concept of Christian social theory, people make pronouncements about particular practical problems, social and national issues. The Free Church Superintendent may speak of bingo as a social scourge; a Roman Catholic Archbishop may say: 'We couldn't do without it'; the Anglican priest may say: 'I leave it to the Parochial Church Council.'

My overall criticism of this first view then is that it moves from an over-simplified theology by a logically hazardous path to reach (not surprisingly) the most

[1] Cp. George S. Hendry's book, *The Gospel of the Incarnation*, a theological protest against fragmentation.

bewildering and apparently conflicting conclusions. And if it be said, 'But "in theory" it's surely all right'—what does this mean? *If* we had a completely comprehensive theology, if we had elaborated detailed reliable connections between metaphysical and sociological assertions, if in other words we were well-nigh omniscient—of course it would be all right! But those conditions are available only to God and not even the most skilled theologian is God, though on this view some would have to speak as if they were, or at least as if they were in heaven—where we shall not be bothered about Christian strategy anyway.

Lest you think all this is too generalized a criticism, may I take Reinhold Niebuhr as a particular illustration of the difficulties which may be encountered on this type of approach. I yield to no one in recognizing that Niebuhr is exceptionally alert to social issues, has a sensitive social conscience and penetrating insight. We can also admire his courage and honesty in changing his mind on social issues, e.g. very likely on pacificism, perhaps, too, on Marxism. But that reflection leads me precisely to the point of my illustration. Niebuhr's distinctive theology focuses (let us say) on the 'claim of love'. This is his key-phrase, guaranteed, sacrosanct—and around this phrase he develops his discussion of social issues concerning democracy, pacificism, race relations, and so on. But the crucial question is: are the two areas ever linked? In what kind of way does he argue from 'the claim of love' to what has to be said and done in a concrete situation about a strike, or testing of nuclear bombs? Not the least merit of a recent study of *The Thought of Reinhold Niebuhr* by Gordon Harland is that it shows quite clearly the kind of phrase used by Niebuhr to make the transition. The 'claim of love' gives (Niebuhr says) a 'vantage point' for making a social judgment, 'finds an embodiment in' such a judgment.

Alternatively, Niebuhr speaks of theology and sociology as 'two dimensions' having a 'dialectical relation' with each other, or even sharing 'tangents of meaning'. More generally still, Niebuhr would say that theology provided 'illumination' for the making of political judgments. It is only fair to say that Mr. Harland, who has obviously made a much more intensive study of Niebuhr than I have ever done, claims that Niebuhr's 'theological and political thought form one consistent whole'.[1] I entirely agree that Niebuhr does try to relate Christian faith and social responsibility, but how far are logical connections established—how far is there a consistent whole?

Indeed, will our theology of society *ever* be developed in this linear fashion?—with social duties given at the outposts of some vast system of theological discourse? Whenever we are tempted to see theology and social judgments as parts of a single system, the judgment of Sir David Ross on Aristotle's politics comes appropriately to mind:

'His political views form part of a large and well-knit system of thought. But sometimes the use made of general principles is somewhat arbitrary, and we feel that they are put forward as reasons for holding beliefs which Aristotle would have held in any case.'[2] Or again: 'It is, though regrettable, not surprising that Aristotle should regard as belonging to the nature of things an arrangement which was so familiar a part of everyday Greek life as slavery was.'[3] This is what inevitably happens when practice falls necessarily short of promise and expectation: we are offered a mere patchwork of principles and prejudice. Certainly we do not make a Christian sociology merely by infiltrating into theological discourse social generalizations which anyone might make, still less by surrounding with a theological frame the social prejudices (Left or Right) of

[1] *loc. cit.* Introduction, p. x.   [2] *Aristotle*, pp. 236-7.   [3] *loc. cit.* p. 241.

D

our own days. In all such cases the connections will inevitably be more psychological and sociological than logical.

Those who view Christian social theory in this first way —with what we have called the 'linear-systematic' approach—inevitably finish with precisely such a logical patchwork, with a ramshackle old building indeed compared with the steel and structure system of their pipedream. Here is one view of a Christian social policy, and on such a view, as we have seen, certainties are reached by various disreputable devices, of which I mention only three:

1. Theological over-simplification: in selecting some principles, perhaps only one, and taking even these in a limited context.

2. Carelessness in argument—confounding inference and psychological association, or inference and mere consistency, or even supposing lack of clear inconsistency to be the same as positive implication.

3. Empirical over-simplification—of the situation to be judged.

This is what happens when Christian social duty is sought in terms of absolute prescriptions, clear leads, definite policies! Here are systematic attempts to formulate Christian social theory, and either they never succeed (which is what is mercifully most often the case) or, when they do, they suffocate the life out of Christian behaviour. Is this the way to be sure in Christian sociology?

Let us rather look at the matter from a different perspective altogether, what we have called the 'empirical-exploratory' approach, one which better accords with our reflections in Chapter I, and one which happens to preserve, as I hope presently to show, some of Maurice's best insights. I propose to elucidate this second concept of Christian social thinking, in four movements:

1. We begin with some social problem as it presents

itself to us in some concrete situation: with the questions which cluster, e.g. around race relations; industrial strikes; nuclear warfare; capital punishment. The first need is to get the issues as clearly explicated as possible, and here there is need for every kind of expert help and co-operation. Here is a task in which sociologists, economists, physicists, prison workers, judges, moralists also join, and where the theologian's main task is to pick up questions.

2. Now the very language and issues raised in such a discussion will echo and suggest certain biblical, especially New Testament, narratives; it may echo certain doctrinal positions, certain classical discussions in the Fathers or Scholastics. The theologian's primary task is to be expert in his own field, and to bring into play *not* one or two choice passages, or some particular slogan of a Reformation or counter-Reformation, *but* all and every element in the Christian dispensation that can be grist to the mill. What is the point? To create just a babble? To weigh everyone down with a heap of learning as Maurice might have said?[1] No: for assuming that, or in so far as, these biblical narratives and classical references were themselves interlocked with a contemporary culture and social pattern, and in this wider context had their point, then there is reason to hope that this original point may now break in on us as we bring alongside our own particular situation. We may then, using an obvious model, talk of God speaking to us in our own day. If we may use a chemical metaphor, it is as though our present social concerns found in the biblical narratives wherein they have been steeped, a speck of an earlier culture and social concern from which contemporary Christian insight could be precipitated. But even now the process is not complete.

[1] See, e.g., his criticism of Ward in *Thoughts on the Rule of Conscientious Subscription*, p. 39.

3. This insight (if it occurs, and it is not ours to command, but God's to give) will show itself in some decision, some forthright judgment on the particular problem or issue under examination, and any such judgment will exhibit *pro tem.* a moral or social Christian principle'— here will be God's message, if we wish to continue the model we used in (2).

4. But the process never ends: the very social judgment brought to bear on the empirical situation will develop and modify it, and as likely as not raise other questions and issues. These will then need, in turn, to be brought again into relation with the biblical and doctrinal narrative, until some other insight is generated, and other principles enunciated. So the process repeats itself.

In this way there is a constant generation of principles, a constant rhythm of insight and generalization, a discipline of exploration. Here is the means by which the Holy Spirit ever guides us into new truth. The Church is not a superior bunch of back-room boys set above society and dispensing 'the answers' to any and all social (let alone intellectual) problems. Nor has it private access to a divine tape-recording. Still less does it provide a kind of programmed machine ready to dispense cut-and-dried answers in the slot. On this view, Christian social theory, or better, Christian social theorizing, is essentially a task for a team. It arises from a meeting of disciplines, where the common search for truth which unites the scientist with his fellows, is fulfilled in a Christian κοινωνία, and where the Christian κοινωνία is humble, generous, charitable enough to see in the fellowship of scientific inquiry a practical expression of itself.[1]

Here is a view which does full justice to the empirical complexity of current social problems, and in its suspicion

[1] Cp. M. B. Foster, *Mystery and Philosophy*, p. 67.

of systems as well as in its God-centredness it preserves the notable insights of a F. D. Maurice. But (it might be said) does it lead to any generalizations worth making? Does it give us any lead at all? All I can do to answer that question is to give one or two large-scale generalizations made on the basis of such insight as comes to me from a union of a highly imperfect knowledge of the biblical narrative with only a partial understanding of contemporary issues. But (as we have already noted) even $\frac{22}{7}$ need not be despised as an approximation for π. My reflections in this matter fall into two parts.

I. A general reflection.

Christian behaviour (like the Christian faith itself) will never be static in the way that, for example, a Huxley or a Hoyle supposes. If our broad position is correct, there will not only be the *possibility* of reform. Reform will be a logical *necessity*. So the Christian can never practise social contentment: since that would presuppose a final systematic pattern completely expressive of Christian insight. The Church is the only social agency bound *in principle* to be reforming, spontaneous and creative, and when the Church ceases to be that, it is dead indeed. As Maurice said: 'God's Church cannot be a lifeless, stationary thing.'[1] The Church must treasure no particular sociological pattern— for that would be idolatry. It treasures a pattern only because and when that pattern enshrines an insight. But it is of the very nature of God-given insight to have logically inadequate because ever reformable expressions. It is true that religion has often been associated (at least in part) with conservatism in thought and practice.[2] But we must

[1] *Thoughts on the Rule of Conscientious Subscription*, p. 38.

[2] Cp. A. N. Whitehead, *Adventures of Ideas* (1933), p. 22: 'On the whole, well-established religious institutions are to be reckoned among the conservative forces of society', though he adds, 'But the ultimate ideals, of

take care that such conservatism does not arise from a mistaken idea that religious insights can be translated into guaranteed and guaranteeing expressions and institutions. The Christian must be the first to agree with D. L. Munby in his book *God and the Rich Society*, 'In a changing world . . . we have to be flexible . . . and such flexibility requires that institutions should never be allowed to exist merely because they have secured a function in the past.'[1] No social system can be so good as not to need improvement. And here (may I say) is the place for genuine constructive Christian controversy. Take, e.g., those in favour of, and those against, capital punishment, or nuclear warfare. Such conflicting moral judgments should be a spur to a *further exploration*—whether of the bible or of the empirical circumstances. The important point is that they are not logical incompatibles, as they would be if each was a conclusion without a deductive system. Each is (at best) the translation of an insight, which occurs when a Christian pattern is brought to bear creatively on a situation of empirical complexity, a translation into such behaviour as seems appropriate to the particular problem which initiated the Christian exercise. Like all translations it can be improved.

II. Now, a more particular reflection.

If I were to hazard any more particular and contemporary large-scale generalization it would fix on what I discern

which they profess themselves the guardians, are a standing criticism of current practices.' Cp. also his *Religion in the Making* (1927), p. 130: 'A system of dogmas may be the ark within which the Church floats safely down the flood-tide of history. But the Church will perish unless it opens its window and lets out the dove to search for an olive branch'; and *Science and the Modern World* (1933), p. 27, where he remarks that while religious 'principles may be eternal', yet 'the expression of the principles requires critical development'.

[1] *loc. cit.* p. 129. Compare his emphasis at p. 177 that it is the mission of the Church to *transform* (italics mine).

as a feature common to various problems of our contemporary society. All our antagonisms—whether within or between nations—thrive when opponents are regarded not as persons, still less as 'joint heirs with Christ',[1] but as impersonal units. Here is a feature displayed by many circumstances of our industrial and commercial life.

Trade Unions, whose fellowship was once grounded in the Gospel, are now often just one more set of committees —or more ominously one more set of 'pressure groups'. They often become in this way depersonalized agencies. Again, automation, while an industrial necessity, *may well be* (though *not* necessarily) a personal disaster. From another direction, may I quote some remarks of Mr. John Marsh, Director of the Industrial Welfare Society, to the Annual Conference of the Churches' Council of Healing, October 1961:

Fundamentally, workers in industry need the maintenance of a reasonable standard of living, a status in society, and intrinsic satisfaction in work. Much attention has been paid to the first of these, but more often than not there is no challenge to a man to give of his best to his work. People are often highly paid to do very little, and failure to use them as human beings is compensated by high wages. Many highly paid managers and executives fail to obtain any satisfaction from their work.

Modern conditions of work can well compromise personal status, and atrophy creative activity. Work in the Old Testament may be a curse, but the Christian must see it as yet another activity to be redeemed by the grace of God, in which the Christian is to find life abundant and eternal, a joint heritage with Christ, the redemption of his personality, and fellowship with God alike in the delicate negotiation of the board room or in the forthright quips of the shop floor of the foundry.

[1] Romans viii. 17.

Where most thinking needs to be done is on how to translate this vision of the person into our industrial and social life. Let us *not* rush in to deny, from ignorance mixed with obscurantism, the need for pressure groups, automation and the like. Our task is to emphasize the need for vision and to show how to preserve vision in the most novel situations. That reflection leads to one more. It is often said (I have implied it myself earlier in this chapter) that Christian sociology reaches today conclusions which liberal-minded humanitarians reached yesterday, if not the day before. But with this second approach to Christian social thinking there can be no such criticism. While Christians will undoubtedly support all sociological developments which lead to an enrichment of man's life, they will even more seriously regard it as their distinctive duty to seek for characteristic patterns which more evidently and less ambiguously preserve Christian insights. Man has not to be a routine-bound moron, and he is no less routine-bound because the routine is colourful and complex and his life in that sense the 'richer'. The man who does the sparkling round of boards, receptions, sherry parties, conferences, trade tours, may have a much more colourful— 'richer'—existence than the girl who puts wrappers round bars of soap. But to admit that, does not imply that personal fulfilment in a Christian sense is necessarily more realized in the one case than the other. It must be the function of a Christian sociology to work out the most diverse patterns in which this fulfilment is most possible, and that is *not* done by any rule of thumb deductions. There is plainly no easy certainty here and no finalities. Christian sociology must always be seeking new social patterns. We must not spend our time or evaporate our energies in defending a past which only too often may be ossified: let us rather make sure that future patterns express

and preserve insights as many past patterns once did.
I have said on a number of occasions that this view
accords with some of Maurice's most characteristic judgments—and it is time that I substantiated that suggestion,
which I will do in four brief points, which will show how
Maurice echoes our own reflections.

1. For Maurice, the basis of Christian sociology is God's
disclosure in Christ—that which is God's Kingdom, Rule,
Sovereign power. It does not reside in a systematic theology. 'Christ came to establish a Kingdom, not to proclaim
a set of opinions. Every man entering into this Kingdom
becomes interested in all its relations, members, circumstances, he cannot separate himself in any wise from them:
he cannot establish a life or interest apart from theirs.'[1] This
is the basis on which 'a Churchman must be a politician'.[2]

2. Certainly we need to translate our insights—'the
Kingdom of Christ' which we discern in the bible-narra-
tives—into some kind of social organization and pattern.
But these social organizations always risk 'individualizing'
—depersonalizing—the person, and the more complex the
society the even greater effort which is demanded on our
part to maintain the vision.

'I am more and more convinced,' wrote Maurice to
R. C. Trench in 1835, 'that we must not use *personal* and
individual as synonymous words: but that in fact we shall
have most sense and lively realization of our distinct personality when we cease to be individuals, and most delight
to contemplate ourselves as members of one body in one
Head.'[3] Once, in days past, there was a pattern in society
which could be supposed (rightly or wrongly) to display

[1] *Kingdom of Christ*, III. 387, quoted by Vidler, *loc. cit.* pp. 197, 196
respectively.
[2] *Ibid.*
[3] *Letters and Memorials of R. C. Trench* (1888), i, 190, quoted by Vidler,
loc. cit. p. 177.

the manifold grace of God shared by its members. What we need to do today is to match rapid social change with our religious insights, to effect some Christian social pattern which unites grace and nature, and does not neglect either the transcendent or the human aspects of personality. Christian sociology needs to preserve a God-centred humanism, it needs to emphasize the transcendent character of human personality, giving to man cosmic significance and cosmic responsibilities; and the fatal condemnation of a Christian sociology will be that it ignores this. For even pagan humanisms (said Maurice) have had a transcendent reference:

May not Epictetus and Marcus Aurelius have perceived something much higher than the word Stoicism can express—an actual governing principle for the life, not a congeries of opinions to be maintained against all challengers? May not the Humanity which the Comtist dreams of be much more to him than all his Positivism, than all the volumes which set it forth? Believing that the true centre of Humanity is He whom all Christian teachers and Societies have professed to acknowledge, I must feel their delinquencies more than that of other men, in so far as they have fallen into Inhumanity.[1]

How much, then, should the Christian make sure that he is adequately sensitive, obedient to his heavenly vision.

I am sure a person may be very benevolent, may have a great general sympathy with those whose misery he actually beholds, and yet may, day after day, go from one tradesman in Regent Street, or Oxford Street, to another without even entertaining the thought that human hands have actually been concerned in the making of the goods which he buys, and that very bitter human tears may have been shed over them in the process.[2]

[1] *Social Morality* (1869), pp. ix–x.
[2] *Reasons for Co-operation* (1851), pp. 8–9.

To generalize the point: the basic criticism of war, not least scientific warfare, as of industrialism is this 'loss of manhood'. 'I am not afraid', said Maurice with astounding foresight and courage, 'that this appetite for slaughter should be strengthened by the scientific contrivances for effecting it of which our age has been prolific.'[1] 'No gift of science is itself a curse, though every one may become a curse.'[2] What needs to be feared, and what the Church must condemn, is the regimentation—the 'individualizing' —of personality which war, and much else, involves. Of all social and political activity, war is that activity where the risk of compromising and degrading persons is greatest.

Here then is the main task of our Christian sociology—to make possible a due reverence for man and his calling. Co-operation and fellowship should be on the basis of Christian insights into human nature, into men's common status as stewards of the manifold grace of God. 'The doctrine that men should call nothing their own was proclaimed by Galilean fishermen before it was adopted into the English Constitution, or gave an impulse to the thought of modern Frenchmen.'[3] 'It worked from the first as a truth, and a power, not as a read rule. It worked in that way all through the corruption, superstition and violence of the Middle Ages. It is working in that way in England at the present time.'[4]

3. So maxims and principles must be living, not dead, and their test must be in action. 'The test of all principles affecting to be moral and human must be in their application to the circumstances in which we are placed.'[5] 'It is well for us to be reminded that all our principles must be tested at last by what they can do for our own characters

---

[1] *Social Morality*, p. 217.   [2] *Ibid.*, p. 217.
[3] *Reasons for Co-operation*, p. 23.   [4] *Ibid.*, p. 23.
[5] *Social Morality*, p. 434.

and for mankind.'[1] So the Christian wages 'implacable war' against 'sectarianism which rends humanity asunder'[2] and against 'imperialism which would substitute for Universal fellowship a Universal death'.[3]

4. Finally, worship is that in which families, social groups, nations, are to find their true bond. 'Worship then I conceive becomes the link between Physical and Moral Studies.'[4] 'So there will be discovered beneath all the politics of the Earth, sustaining the order of each country, upholding the charity of each household, a City which has foundations, whose builder and maker is God.'[5]

Here is Maurice's own approach to that co-operative venture which we called the empirical-exploratory version of Christian sociology; and with it goes his condemnation of deductive systematizing.

And now at the end someone may protest: does Maurice, or do I, anything more than Niebuhr to connect religious and sociological assertions? I will not try to answer for Maurice. Let me only comment that my own position differs from that of Niebuhr in two ways:

1. I have suggested that, faced with contemporary social problems, both theological and sociological considerations must be so developed as to reveal their various presuppositions, and the expectation, at least of the Christian, is that this common task and inquiry will lead towards a common worship wherein these presuppositions are jointly anchored, and wherein the research group comes to know the fellowship of the Holy Spirit guiding men into all the truth. *Logically* this implies that theological language and sociological language can be shown each to have presuppositions which themselves can be linked by assertions

---

[1] *Social Morality*, p. 430.   [2] *Ibid.*, pp. 482–3.
[3] *Ibid.*, pp. 482–3.   [4] *Ibid.*, pp. 479–80.
[5] *Ibid.*, p. 482.

containing the integrator word 'God'.[1] It is at that point that I would hint at 'metaphysical' links which go (I believe) beyond Niebuhr.[2] On the other hand, I am quite prepared to hear it said that Niebuhr could interpret his metaphors in a way that would support my view, e.g. to speak of 'tangents of meaning' shared by theology and sociology presumably implies differences which may not exclude logical connections along the tangents (Fig. B); again, to talk of different 'dimensions' only excludes a common origin of reference if the lines are completely skew. Otherwise, different dimensions, represented as they usually are by three lines as axes, meet in a common point, the origin, O (Fig. C).

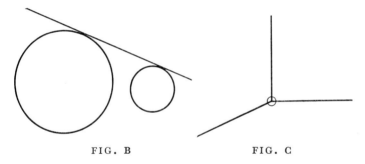

FIG. B   FIG. C

2. But Niebuhr seems to suppose that theology is quite static, so that all that may change are the sociological implications. It is basic, however, to my position, that the

---

[1] For some elucidation of this suggestion perhaps I may refer the reader to what I have said elsewhere, e.g. *Prospect for Metaphysics* (edited I. T. Ramsey), ch. x, 'On the possibility and purposes of a metaphysical theology.'

[2] I emphasize that this is *not* to say that even in theory a *deductive* Christian sociology is possible. For a presupposition in this sense is not an axiom: and I think (as I said) that the basic mistake of the other, linear systematic, view of Christian social theory is to think of theology as a deductive system. The wild goose of a Cartesian method ever leads men to false expectations.

theological assertions to which the Christian insight which is generated by the social problems gives rise, *cannot* be specified as infallible posits. All that is 'static' is (to use Niebuhr's models) the common tangent or the origin respectively—*not* the circles, *nor* the axes: all that is 'static' is God. In the diagrams below, the different circles suggest the increasing spread of our sociological and theological maps as our sociological and theological understandings develop (Fig. D). The different axes may be taken to represent different logical directions in which inquiries within any one field (whether sociology or theology) may proceed.[1] (Fig. E.)

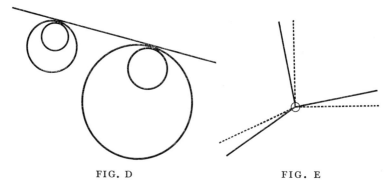

FIG. D   FIG. E

Does this emphasis on development mean, however, that we must always think of reformulating theology? Cannot we be sure about the Creeds? Or the Articles? If not, what does the poor clergyman do about the Articles? After all (it may be said) he has to subscribe to them. Well,

[1] It may be that the model of dimensions is less clear than that of the circles, and the reader may wonder why both are used. My reason is a very general one, and I gladly declare it. I think that more frequently, rather than less, ought we to develop the models which occur in theological reasoning to see how far they offer possibilities of genuine illumination, to see whether they are as meritorious as they are sometimes uncritically supposed to be.

what do we mean by 'being sure' about the Creeds or Articles? Do we have here some sacrosanct expressions? Those are the kinds of questions to occupy us in the next chapter.

Meanwhile, I have argued that we can be sure of our Christian social duty, that we can be sure of God's demand, without ever being certain about any social pronouncement into which that duty is translated and expressed. And if this puzzles or worries the reader, reflect that it is in fact often the case with all our duty. As Professor Maclagan remarks in a recent book: 'To insist on dutifulness is not in itself to say anything as to what our specific duties are.'[1] Being sure in religion does not entail being certain in theology; to be aware of our Duty does not necessarily give us an infallible prescription. Let us as Christians be ready to acknowledge that it is at once a measure of our status and the source of our inspiration, first, that we are finite, and then, that Christian morality with all its reformable pronouncements is a permanent adventure, moving when it is faithful, as Maurice would say, into light.

[1] *The Theological Frontier of Ethics*, p. 97.

III

SUBSCRIPTION TO ARTICLES

In Chapter I, I showed how Maurice's treatment of 'eternal punishment' displayed two features typical of his whole position. Positively, Maurice was sure of God, and it was (we said) as a means of disclosing God's Charity that the phrase 'eternal punishment' had to be used. On the other hand, and negatively, Maurice was suspicious of all theological schemes, of all systems whose verbal rigour concealed rather than revealed God. Sure in religion— but suspicious of all theological pretensions. Ironically enough it was Dr. Jelf, the Principal of King's College when Maurice resigned, who in a letter to Maurice dated 14 July 1853[1] had said that 'so far as attempting to fathom the mystery' (of eternity and eternal punishment) goes 'it seems to me the less said the better'. Wise words, but Maurice was compelled to retort two months later, in September 1853, 'Nevertheless, you enter into a very elaborate "controversial argument" on this subject in the course of which more attempts are made to fathom the mystery than I should have thought at all desirable.' While Maurice worshipped the mystery, he was rightly suspicious of all theological claims to have mapped it to the last detail.

We saw in Chapter II how this same antithesis between intuitive conviction and systematic certainty, between

[1] *The word 'Eternal' and the Punishment of the Wicked.* Correspondence printed Cambridge, 1854.

insight and system, between the discernment of a mystery and our theological understanding of it, repeats itself in two diverse views of Christian social theory. We must certainly ground our social judgments in such disclosures as we have of God and his sovereign power, we must match them with such insights as we have into the Kingdom of Christ—there is our sure basis for Christian social theory. But let us not profess to reach Christian social duties as the certain conclusions of a theological system. As an attempt to chart a mystery, Christian social theory must be intrinsically tentative, ever open to reform and modification—striving at all times to be faithful alike to our vision of God as to our deepest insights into human personality.

Being sure in religion—but cautious, tentative, approximate in theology. In this Chapter I hope to show more clearly what I have in mind by speaking of a tentative theology, and to do this by considering in particular what we mean by being certain of the Creeds and the Thirty-Nine Articles.

We might suppose that we could guess already Maurice's attitude to the Creeds and the Articles. Too much system here, you might think, to please Maurice; tentative in theology—so: exeunt the Creeds, preceded by the Thirty-Nine Articles. It might seem as if Maurice would have said: 'Hang theology, let's just be Christian.' Or, as the old chorus had it: 'The Religion of Paul and Silas, the Religion of Paul and Silas, the Religion of Paul and Silas, it's good enough for me.' But for good or ill, Paul did more than sing hymns with Silas: he wrote theological epistles to the Galatians and to the Romans (to mention no other). To be tentative in theology must not mean that we virtually dispense with theology altogether: that is far too facile an account of theological caution, and too easy

E

an answer for Maurice as well. For recall that in 1835 he wrote *Subscription No Bondage, or, The Practical Advantages afforded by the Thirty-Nine Articles as guides in all the branches of Academical Education*,[1] following this ten years later by *Thoughts on the Rule of Conscientious Subscription, on the purpose of the Thirty-nine Articles, and on our present perils from the Romish system*.

S. C. Carpenter, writing of Maurice in *Church and People*, says: 'His friends, Mill and Carlyle, could not think why, at a time when so many were "emancipating themselves from the chains of dogma", Maurice could take positive delight in binding himself to Creeds, and even to Articles.'[2]

Why was Maurice so sure about the Creeds and Articles? Where was Maurice's tentative theology now? Can anyone be so sure as to repeat *ex animo* Creeds, and subscribe *ex animo* to Articles? Or was Maurice after all (in Leslie Stephen's words) 'muddle-headed . . . futile . . . utterly bewildering'.[3] Behind all these questions is a more fundamental one: *how* are we to be tentative in theology? What sort of theological caution is a virtue? That (as I have said) is the question for our attention in this chapter, and one which I propose to discuss by reference to the Creeds, the Articles and the concept of theological subscription.

Belief in the Creeds and Articles—what sort of belief is it? May I begin by adapting a story William Temple once told?[4] Suppose someone comes up to us in the office, the laboratory or the library, just when we are concentrating on balancing that account, or doing that tricky titration, or worrying out that puzzling paragraph, and says: 'Is Charlie about?' Or, to take a more domestic example,

---

[1] Hereafter referred to as *Subscription No Bondage*.
[2] *loc. cit.* (1937 edition), p. 528.
[3] Quoted by A. R. Vidler, *loc. cit.* p. 4.
[4] In a sermon in St. Mary's, Cambridge, about 1935.

suppose we ask our wife, busy preparing a meal—'Did I leave my slippers by the side of the fire this morning?' In the concentration of the moment, and with only a passing concern, the reply, if it is charitable, may be: 'Yes, I believe so!' 'I believe so' ='I haven't given it much thought, and for various reasons I don't intend to— there are other and more important claims on my time— but if I did, that is probably, though not inevitably, the conclusion to which the evidence would lead.' 'I believe so.' Is this what we mean by religious belief? No parallel here you'll say, to our attitude to the Creeds and Articles, however tentative. But listen to a passage from the report of the Oxford University Commission of 1852, referring to the different interpretations of the assent to the Thirty-nine Articles, then required of undergraduates on matriculation, which were given by different vice-chancellors and pro-vice-chancellors at the time of the subscription: 'Sometimes the person matriculated is told that "he hereby expresses his assent to the Thirty-Nine Articles, so far as he knows them"; sometimes that "he probably has not read them, but that he has no objection to them"; sometimes that "he thereby declares himself ['on the side' so to speak] to be a member of the Church of England". Sometimes, however, no observation is made.'[1] Formulate the parallels to such questions as: 'Is Charlie about?' 'Did I leave my slippers by the side of the fire this morning?' The answer 'I believe so' translates: (a) 'Yes, as far as I know', (b) 'I've not given it a thought, but I see no reason to think he's not (or you didn't)', (c) 'I don't know, but I want to be pally.' . . . Or (d) is it wisest to make no observation whatever? Here are various ways of being far too tentative in theology. . . . *How* then are we to be *justifiably* tentative?

[1] *Report of the Oxford University Commission of 1852*, p. 55.

As a preliminary to answering that question, let us first refresh our minds on the general character of the Creeds and Articles. Let us begin with the Ethiopian eunuch of Acts viii, reading his bible, and in particular Isaiah liii, and being joined by Philip. What Philip did (we are told) was, 'beginning from this Scripture', to preach Jesus. In other words, he brought the pattern of the Suffering Servant alongside the passion and death of Jesus Christ in such a way as to generate insight, to effect a disclosure . . . which is *something like* what occurs when two similar pictures—not exactly the same to be sure—on being brought together are suddenly seen in a new dimension, and the whole circumstance comes to life. The Suffering Servant and Jesus: the two pictures were brought together to generate a disclosure, and we read that the eunuch believed and was baptized. Now you will recall that according to an additional verse in some MS. the eunuch, to give proof that he believed with all his heart, uttered what is one of the most primitive forms of a Christian creed: 'I believe that Jesus Christ is the Son of God.'[1] The interest for us is that here was a Credal assertion which the eunuch judged to be an apt expression for what had been disclosed to him by Philip's preaching, for what had called forth his response and commitment. Here is the eunuch, sure in religion, explicit in theology. Likewise St. Paul, writing to the Church of Corinth (I Cor. xv) could recall 'the gospel which I preached to you', by reciting what is plainly a catena of credal phrases: 'I delivered unto you . . . that which also I received, how that Christ died for our sins according to the Scriptures, and that he was buried, and that he hath been raised on the third day according to the Scriptures.'[2] So credal phrases—embedded in the Scriptures—were regarded as apt and reliable currency for

[1] Acts viii. 37.   [2] I Cor. xv. 3, 4.

Christian commitment. This is obviously true of the earliest creeds which were, as is well known, baptismal creeds, of which our Apostles' Creed is not untypical. These Creeds originated, we may remember, in answer to questions preceding baptism, and such answers were (so to say) cue-phrases which were meant to carry with them all that the catechumen had been taught: which were meant in other words to incorporate a whole background of teaching— and one which was essentially Scriptural. This was implied in the *redditio symboli* following as a response to the *traditio symboli*. In this way the creeds proclaimed a faith, when all their phrases were rooted in the gospel, so that the Creed became expressive of a response to that transcendent challenge which the Gospels express. So, appropriately, credal questions were not of the form: Do you believe that so-and-so is the case? which is like: Is Charlie in fact in? Or, were my slippers in fact there? But they were of the form: do you believe in God, in Jesus Christ? which is more like: do you believe in, do you trust Charlie? Or, to my wife, do you trust me? Even the concentration on ledgers, titrations, chapters or cooking, would stop for that.

But, baptismal creeds apart, what of a conciliar creed, such as that which we call the Nicene Creed? What of a creed including phrases like 'being of one substance with the Father'? Are not such phrases altogether more philosophical, calling for learned appraisal, theological detachment? How can they express a sure devotion and commitment? To answer that question let us see how in fact these conciliar Creeds arose, and what is their logical point. Political pressures, private jealousies and ecclesiastical rivalries apart, our so-called Nicene Creed arose from an attempt to bring order and consistency into Christian thinking, not least when an appeal to the Scriptures brought apparently conflicting phrases. E.g. the apostle

Thomas might call Jesus 'My Lord and my God',[1] but is this consistent with talk of Jesus as 'God's son'? To be a son, said Arius, is in the last resort to be subordinate to a father. Again, is the apostle's profession consistent with John xiv. 28: 'My Father is greater than I'? In such ways, a scriptural phrase might be misleading in isolation, and certainly would not normally by itself be adequate. Scriptural phrases may be not plainly consistent with each other. Hence there arises the need to order biblical phrases by forging consistency-links, and for some of these links men needed to look elsewhere. To settle disputes about Scriptural phrases there came the need to look for another sort of authority—that of reason—and in this way the philosophical language of the day provided the needed elucidation. For example—'I believe in Jesus Christ'. Certainly, he was a historical figure: a man who wept, who was hungry, who was crucified, suffered and buried. But to cope as well with utterances like those of the apostle Thomas, to allow for insights into the cosmic Christ, these historical phrases came to be balanced by others, by phrases from current philosophy which not only provided a consistent frame in which to set the biblical phrases but whose logic was peculiar enough to make their transcendent point; philosophical phrases such as: 'being of one substance with the Father', 'by whom all things were made'. In this way we may see the conciliar Creeds uniting natural and revealed religion, being essays in the full and consistent expression of Christian commitment. No need to think of them as descriptive blueprints of the life of God. If only the matter had rested there. . . .

But, as Cranmer said of Common Prayer: 'There was never anything by the wit of man so well devised, or so sure established, which in continuance of time hath not

[1] John xx. 28.

been corrupted . . .'[1] and as we all know, very diverse structures were built out from the Creeds, so that by the time of the Reformation the primitive theological paradise had proliferated into a veritable jungle. There were Articles of various numbers. Between the ten of 1536, and the thirty-nine of 1571, came at one time or another, thirteen, forty-two and thirty-eight. In this way there were diverse Articles and diverse numbers of Articles, all claiming to afford further guidance to the theological traveller.

It was in 1628 that Laud advised Charles I to reprint the Thirty-nine Articles with a preface which he hoped would bring to an end controversies then raging—'curious and unhappy differences'—and in particular would make it plain that the Articles were not Calvinistic propaganda. The interest for us is that in controversy about the Articles theology was being supposed so tentative as to allow every man to have the interpretation he fancied. At the same time the Preface claimed (on what grounds we need not ask) that 'all clergymen within our Realm' agree in 'the *true, usual, literal* meaning of the said Articles', and declared that 'no man hereafter shall either print, or preach, to draw the Article aside any way, but shall submit to it in the *plain and full* meaning thereof: or shall not put his own sense or comment to be the meaning of the Article, but shall take it in the *literal and grammatical* sense.' (Italics mine.) Here was a formula, then, whose language was to be taken in its plain and full meaning, in its literal and grammatical sense. Further, subscription was in no uncertain terms. Going back to the 36th Canon of 1604 and 'for avoiding of all ambiguities' subscription had to be in this order and form of words: 'I, N N, do willingly and *ex animo* subscribe . . . to all things that are contained

[1] *Concerning the Service of the Church.* Preface to the English Prayer Book of 1549.

therein'; and the 51st Canon had made it clear that a man, on pain of excommunication must neither affirm that the Thirty-nine Articles are 'superstitious or erroneous' nor deny that he can 'with a good conscience subscribe thereunto'. Nothing tentative here: but already for us a difficulty begins to show itself. Do we subscribe to plain literal senses 'from the heart'—as *ex animo* came to be rendered in the diverse forms of subscription current after 1688? Are plain, flat assertions ever the kind of assertion to which *ex animo* subscription can be given? Do we confess from the heart, e.g. that Queen Anne is dead? Do plain meanings raise any questions of conscience? Further, is a plain meaning a full meaning? But those questions anticipate.

We may grant that the Thirty-nine Articles do not easily and exactly fit into a Calvinistic frame. But equally clearly they did not drop ready-made from some heavenly teleprinter. In their turn, they go back to Scripture, and the formulae of traditional doctrine. Indeed, even His Majesty's Declaration of 1628 talked of 'the *general*[1] meaning of the Articles of the Church of *England*' in relation to the Holy Scriptures, wherein would be found 'God's promises' in which all disputes could be shut up. Is there, then, a '*general*' meaning besides a usual, full and 'plain' meaning?

Now, whatever problems this diversity of adjectives raises, and at some of them we look presently, at least it is clear already that to understand the Articles it was not supposed to be enough to give the words plain, literal senses. The words must at least be set in a wider context of Scripture and classical doctrine. But the question arises: in what way are these contextual connections to be made —and logical links forged?

[1] Italics mine.

When Dr. Samuel Clarke published his *Scripture Doctrine of the Trinity* in 1712, he claimed that 'every person may reasonably agree to such forms, wherever he can, *in any sense at all*, reconcile them with Scripture'.[1] Waterland opposed such a claim, and in his *Case of Arian Subscription considered and the several pleas and excuses for it particularly examined and confuted* (1721), condemned those who held 'that they could lawfully and conscientiously subscribe to the Articles in any sense in which they themselves, by their own interpretation, can reconcile them to Scriptures, without regard to the meaning and intention, either of the persons who first compiled them or who now impose them'.[2] Gibson complains of this 'dishonest and disingenuous manner of subscribing';[3] and so it was if it led Archdeacon Blackburne to assert 'the inalienable privilege of everyone to believe as he pleases'.[4] Here is tentative theology with a vengeance!

What is undeniable, however, is that *even* if a plain and literal sense be admitted, the contextual setting of the words in relation to the authorities of Scripture and tradition needs still to be worked out before the Articles can be genuinely understood. *From the logical point of view*, Newman in Tract XC[5] was only doing what Samuel Clarke, in another case, had attempted in an earlier age, viz. providing a logical reconciliation between doctrine and Scripture. What of course he did *in fact* was to show that it was not impossible to provide logical links—reliable argument—of such a kind as united the Thirty-nine Articles with doctrines which could be called Catholic if

[1] Quoted by E. C. S. Gibson, *The Thirty-Nine Articles*, p. 63.
[2] Quoted by Gibson, *loc. cit.* p. 63, from Waterland's *Works*, ii, 264.
[3] *loc. cit.* p. 63.
[4] To take a phrase quoted by Gibson, *loc. cit.* p. 63, from a judgment on Blackburne's *Confessional* by G. G. Perry in his *English Church History*, iii, 201.
[5] Published 27 February 1841.

not Roman. In this way, he attempted to show that the Articles were 'patient of a Catholic interpretation'. Not that he did this without a certain amount of ingenuity. For example, the sessions of the Council of Trent which dealt with Purgatory, or the propitiatory sacrifice of the Mass, had not occurred when the relevant Articles were framed: so the Articles could not (he argued) specifically exclude, still less condemn, Tridentine decrees on this subject. The 'Romish doctrine' of Article XXII may thus be no more than the doctrines of the 'medievalist party'; only with such doctrines are the Articles by design logically inconsistent. Again, in the case of Article XXI—we may all agree (he said, in effect) that assemblies of men 'not governed with the Spirit of the Word of God may err, and sometimes have erred, even in things pertaining to God'. But what if 'supernatural privilege' is promised? While Councils are a thing of earth, their infallibility of course is not guaranteed: but when they are a thing of heaven, their deliberations are divinely overruled, so that their decrees are absolutely authoritative.[1] In this way, it is not logically impossible to combine Article XXI with an assertion that Councils (i.e. Heavenly Councils) cannot err. Here are examples of Newman's logical mapwork.

The novelty of Newman's logical reconciliation led the Bishop of Oxford to declare that such treatment as this would 'make the Articles mean anything or nothing', and we are reminded of the comments of Waterland, Blackburne and of Gibson.[2] Undoubtedly, most people believed that the one true meaning of the Articles was some set of incontrovertible facts which the Articles pictured. The

[1] The difficulty of course is to establish criteria for any heavenly councils or for assemblies being governed by the Word of God. (Cp. what is said earlier about desiring on earth the kind of certainty which is more appropriate to heaven—p. 32).

[2] See above, p. 57.

very possibility of contextual interpretations, and the new responsibility of judging between different and various contextual interpretations was hardly, if at all, recognized. A century was to elapse before we heard Wittgenstein's slogan: 'Don't look for meanings, look for use'—a slogan to which we return presently. But Newman may have had an inkling of such points when, some twenty-two years afterwards, he wrote to *The Times*[1] and declared:

> I maintained in Tract XC that the XXXIX Articles ought to be subscribed in their literal and grammatical sense: but I maintained this also: that they were so drawn up as to admit, in their grammatical sense, of subscription on the part of persons who differed very much from each other in the judgment which they formed of Catholic doctrine.

And yet, however slow men were to see the logical points which were involved, nevertheless to claim this broad comprehensiveness, in this sense a contextual tentativeness, for the Thirty-nine Articles, was not new. Archbishop Ussher had written:

> We do not suffer any man to reject the Thirty-nine Articles of the Church of England at his pleasure; yet neither do we look upon them as essentials of saving faith, or legacies of Christ and the Apostles; but [as] a mean, as pious opinions fitted for the preservation of unity; neither do we oblige any man to believe them, but only not to contradict them.[2]

Hensley Henson quotes Chillingworth on the same theme. Chillingworth, Henson says, held that 'subscription to the Thirty-nine Articles meant no more than a general belief in the soundness of the Church of England, and that "there is no error which may necessitate or warrant any

[1] 24 February 1863.
[2] Quoted by H. H. Henson, *The Church of England*, p. 98.

man to disturb the peace and renounce the communion of it".'[1] And Henson continues:

It is certain that the Thirty-nine Articles were in their original intention more politic than theological. The practical wisdom of the Tudor statesmen mitigated the dogmatic ardour of the Tudor divines. Queen Elizabeth was more concerned for civic harmony than for religious orthodoxy. Fuller, writing in the next century, gave a true account of the conditions under which the Anglican Articles were finally shaped: 'Children's clothes ought to be made of the biggest, because afterwards their bodies will grow up to the garments. Thus the articles of the English protestant church, in the infancy thereof, they thought good to draw up in general terms, foreseeing that posterity would grow up to fill the same, I mean, these holy men did prudently prediscover that differences in judgments would unavoidably happen in the church, and were loath to unchurch any, and drive them off from an ecclesiastical communion for such petty differences; which made them pen the articles in comprehensive words, to take in all who, differing in the branches, met in the root of the same religion.'

Fuller was both a peace-maker and a jester. His kindly humorous disposition had little in common with the severity of Puritan habit, and the meticulous intrusiveness of Laudian discipline. But men felt too strongly about their religion to accept metaphors and jokes for arguments. The Anglican children as they grew up found the prudently ample vestures provided for them both ill-fitting and uncomfortable. They looked longingly to the neater garments of Geneva, and the more splendid habiliments of Rome. Accordingly they betook themselves to the arts and crafts of exegetic casuistry, and sought to explain away whatever in the Articles they could not endure.[2]

Even if the Articles were to be given a 'plain and literal sense', it was certainly one which left open their contextual

[1] Henson, *loc. cit.* p. 98, quoting Chillingworth's preface to his *Religion of Protestants*.   [2] Henson, *loc. cit.* pp. 100–1.

elucidation. Connections with Scripture and traditional formulae were apparently not unambiguously given. Fuller might defend the loose contextual fit—but there was always the possibility that the tidy-minded would want to complete the connections, with either the neat severity of Geneva, or the splendid complexity of Rome. The great risk was that the Articles should be contextually so loose as to be impossibly ambiguous.

At any rate, differences of interpretation, of contextual elucidation, however distressing, however unexpected, could not be avoided, and while the Articles might stand victorious against Samuel Clarke's Arianism, Newman's Catholicism left neither Articles nor subscription unmoved. In 1865 the Clerical Subscription Act replaced what Henson has called a 'more precise and stringent formula' —and thus was born the declaration to which all Anglican clergymen are now accustomed:

I assent to the Thirty-nine Articles of Religion and to the Book of Common Prayer, and to the Ordering of Bishops, Priests and Deacons. I believe the Doctrine of the Church of England, as therein set forth, to be agreeable to the Word of God. . . .

I have said so much about the Articles, partly because of Maurice's interest in the Articles and subscription, but also because their history shows us some of the difficulties which arise when we try to be tentative in theology, and it underlines the importance of getting as clear an answer as possible to our definitive question: how may we be justly tentative in theology?

Let us now approach our answer by recalling those phrases which have circulated from the start around the discussion of the Articles: 'plain literal sense, or meaning', 'general sense', 'full sense or meaning'. May I suggest that recent insights into meaning can illuminate these diverse phrases, and may help us to elucidate better the notion of a tentative theology?

Suppose we ask someone: 'What is the meaning of x?' The first point to notice is the possible diversity of the answers, which (as we shall see) enshrines a certain basic ambiguity. Let us take three examples. First, suppose x is a terrific commotion in an undergraduate's room—heat, noise, smoke, jostling. 'What's the meaning of this?' we ask, and the reply comes: 'It's Jim's twenty-first birthday party.' The question in this first example is thus a request for a context, and given the context we are satisfied. Take now a second example. Presented with an integration sign, $\int$, or with $\int y dx$, we may ask: 'What's the meaning of this?' and we may then be told how to use or operate the sign $\int$, or how to work out the expression. Alternatively we might be told: 'It's the area under the curve $y=f(x)$.' Thirdly we may ask: 'What's the meaning of ultramarine?' and this is normally a request to see the colour. The basic ambiguity, which the second example best illustrates in so far as it combines the kinds of answer given respectively in the first and third examples, is between context and reference, and when we speak of the meaning of a word we normally have both in mind. If we are asked: 'What's a copper?' we certainly need to know the context and with the context comes the reference. 'Coppers were brisk,' we read in Stock Exchange Reports when the context is that of shares. 'Put it on the copper,' said the Victorian cook to the kitchen maid. 'Fetch the copper,' says the urchin in Hackney; 'Coppers only,' says the machine in the Tube station.

Now one of the results of contemporary empiricism, and especially of the influence of the later Wittgenstein, has been to emphasize the importance of the contextual setting of words. 'Don't look for meanings, look for use,' was, as we have already noticed, one of his slogans, and if (like all slogans) it is one-sided, no harm to it for that. For its importance is to warn us, and the warning is especially important in theology, *not* to look for descriptive picture-meanings, but to look rather at the context in which a word or phrase is set.

With this in mind let us go back to those curious phrases: 'plain and literal', 'general' and 'full' senses. First 'plain and literal sense'. Now, at first sight, this might seem to be not at all problematical, and it is true that negatively we all know what lies behind any emphasis on it. It is meant to guard against what is in fact intellectual dishonesty, against anyone giving to a word or phrase a completely arbitrary context. It is meant to guard against what Lysicles, in Berkeley's *Alciphron*[1] alleges was a habit of 'the most profound and speculative divines' who (he says)

finding it impossible to reconcile the attributes of God taken in the common sense . . . with human reason and the appearances of things taught that the words knowledge, wisdom, goodness and such-like, when spoken of the Deity, must be understood in a quite different sense from what they signify in the vulgar acceptation. . . .

Insistence on a plain and literal sense is meant to guard against those fanciful interpretations which can make a word mean anything. It is meant to guard against giving to a word a disingenuous arbitrary context. It is meant to guard against typological excess, as well as to guard against those arbitrary inconsistencies such as find their way into legal argument. The Superintendent of Police assures us with a pretence of convincing argument that our car must have been causing an obstruction because (did not Lord

[1] iv, 17.

Goddard give the word this context at the High Court?) no one else could occupy the place which it did. But he does not conclude from this that, giving 'obstruction' the same context, the magistrates are therefore obstructing the Bench. Here is what I mean by a word being given an arbitrary, partial, and therefore misleading context. 'Plain, literal meanings'—here is a phrase which is rightly intended to exclude one possibility of being tentative in theology, which would make theologians no more than disingenuous! Whatever contextual setting is given to a word or phrase, it must not create arbitrary inconsistencies.

But by this time of the day there is another point to be made about 'plain and literal' senses, and I am bound to think it is an even more important point, though it makes us question the value of any emphasis on 'plain and literal' senses in theology, or with reference to the Thirty-nine Articles in particular. Never let us suppose that the 'plain and literal' sense means that we must give the phrases a descriptive logic, the logic *par excellence* of scientific discourse, than which no language could be plainer or more literal. If the Articles were descriptive in this thoroughgoing sense (so that original sin being an 'infection of nature' (Article IX) might call for a Ministry of Health Vaccination Order) they would plainly be devoid of any religious merit, for their anchorage would be wholly in what is given by sense-experience. Any reference to the 'unseen' would be *ex hypothesi* denied. Yet to talk of 'plain and literal' senses must inevitably suggest that theological language is descriptive, when the procession of the Spirit from the Father and the Son (Article V) is supposed to be as plainly and literally a procession as is the Lord Mayor's Show; and to say that Christ has been sitting in Heaven and will do so until he return (Article IV) is to speak as though someone were safely lodged in a deck-chair until he returns for the next meal. Those are descriptive contexts, 'plain and literal senses', making theological words work exactly like 'ultramarine', and they make theology near blasphemy. Let no one blind himself to the sheer atheism to which a 'plain and literal' understanding of theology may lead us. Pastorally, it can be disastrous. I remember as an assistant curate asking a mother about her daughter's confirmation. She replied: 'I certainly want my daughter to be confirmed. When I went to hospital the first thing I was asked was when I'd last been vaccinated, and was I confirmed.' Beyond the point I granted at the start of this particular discussion, I cannot see any merit whatever—on the contrary, I can see immense and disastrous difficulties—in emphasizing a plain and literal sense in relation to theology and the Thirty-nine Articles in particular. This is not to deny of course, that there are some phrases in the Articles which, not being particularly theological, may be given a 'plain and literal' sense, e.g. about the 'Names and number of the Canonical books' (Article VI) or that when given this sense some of these assertions are by now false, e.g. to suppose the *Quicunque Vult* is '*Athanasius's* Creed' (Article VIII), or that the 'Bishop of Rome hath no jurisdiction in this Realm of *England*' (Article XXXVII). But that is another story.

Let us look, however, at some of the other phrases used about our understanding of the Articles, e.g. the 'general' or 'full' sense, and for our purpose we may take these phrases as synonymous. What is their point? On the interpretation I have suggested, their important point is that we must set the Articles in their fullest, most general and most appropriate context. And what context that is, is plain. The Articles are to be understood in a context which links them with the Creeds, and through the Creeds

F

with classical doctrine and the Scriptures.[1] Then, in so far
as and because these logical connections are satisfactorily
traced and mapped, the Articles, like the credal phrases of
Paul, like the profession of the eunuch, find their ground
and defence in, and have for their topic, Christian commitment—the vision of God's love and power in Christ.

Christian Theology is thus to be seen as spreading from
the Bible, in which already it had its first expressions, until
the Creeds emerge as a definitive stage in consistent map-
ping, and supply us with rules to guide subsequent Christian discourse. The Articles then represent (so to say) a
second stage in so far as they endeavour to prescribe what
they judge on this basis to be reliable (and by contrast
unreliable) inferences. In short, they give us (so to say)
and in principle, a specimen context of reliable doctrinal
development which, routed through the Creeds and the
Scriptures, is grounded in a discernment of God.

It is such a way of thinking (I suggest) which lies behind
Maurice's view of the Articles, where a tentative theology
and a distrust of systematic certainty are united with such
devotion as can be expressed in *ex animo* subscription. On
Maurice's view of the Articles, their defence must be that
they are currency for that same disclosure of God in
Christ which the Bible and the Creeds were meant to
speak of.

They may be 'perfectly unlike the Liturgy and Creeds
in form, so that they can never be substituted for them'
but nevertheless, said Maurice, 'they do honour to them as
leading men into an apprehension of a more perfect form
of truth than can by possibility be expressed in dogmatic

[1] e.g. in Article XV the article is explicitly embedded in the words of
Scripture: 'But all we the rest, although baptized, and born again in Christ,
yet offend in many things; and if we say we have no sin, we deceive ourselves, and the truth is not in us.'

language: for no act can be as high as that of Worship; if we know what it means we must know that it is the entrance into a Mystery, into the presence of that Absolute and Eternal Truth, which words may speak of but cannot embody.'[1] In this way the Articles were ultimately to be set in a context of worship. 'Theological articles, placed at the threshold of our studies, would seem by their very name to testify that God, and not Self, is to be the object of our studies as well as of our devotions.'[2]

As that last quotation has implied, the Articles had therefore, for Maurice, high educational value. They were a specimen theological essay grounded in a vision of God, and it was on this ground that he defended the custom of University subscription. Far better to acknowledge, *via* the Articles, that the object of our studies was given in a worshipful disclosure, than to be overwhelmed by verbal systems and to make a fetish of points of view instead. Were the Articles removed, said Maurice, 'our education would lose its meaning, its manliness, its coherency'.[3] But he continued, 'this explanation is grounded upon the assertion, that the Thirty-nine Articles are not terms of communion, but are conditions of thought primarily designed to assist education by warning students against superstitions, which have hindered, and are likely to hinder, the pursuit of knowledge and the attainment of truth'.[4] 'Left to his own caprices in a German University, I believe a young man, very earnest in philological pursuits, is likely sooner or later to become the tenant of a lunatic asylum, unless he should have the more wretched fate of being the founder of some new metaphysical theory.'[5]

[1] *Thoughts on the Rule of Conscientious Subscription*, pp. 12–13.
[2] *Ibid.*, p. 24.
[3] *Subscription No Bondage*, ii.
[4] *Ibid.*, p. 13
[5] *Ibid.*, p. 59.

And what of those who claimed to be content with the bible and to want no Articles and presumably no Creeds; whose tentative attitude to theology arose from a complete distrust of all theological thinking?

What is the real reason why propository Articles were supposed to interfere with the Bible? Because the Bible itself is supposed to be a set of propository Articles. This great fiction, this monstrous insult to the Divine word, has gained ground most extensively in the Protestant Church, and was never more in fashion than in the present day. A more striking defence of Articles than this cannot be produced; those who will not submit their minds to the conditions of thought which grave men, practised in their own hearts and in the history of the world, have composed for their assistance, in order to deliver them out of the notions and superstitions that are natural to their own mind, and which are growing up all around them, these men so find the *want* of such Articles, such conditions of thought, that they turn the book of God, which was written for no such purpose, into a set of formal propositions. And thus it comes to pass, that all the mighty schemes of Providence—all the development of a nation's life through different stages of its history,—all the actual growth of the nation out of the family, of the church out of the nation,—all the living practical records, by which man is made known to himself, to his brother man, and by which God is made known to him,—all the plan of education which God hath pursued to bring man to a knowledge of Himself, and which is set down with such marvellous order and accuracy in that book—all this is forgotten, and thrown overboard by those, who nevertheless claim for *the Bible* the worship *it* claims for God. Under pretence of magnifying the words of Scripture, they destroy the very letter of the book; they will not take plain words to mean words, and acts to mean acts. Every thing is to be sacrificed in order that the book may be converted into a framework of notions and propositions.[1]

[1] *Subscription No Bondage*, pp. 84–5.

So the Articles could (thought Maurice) be our defence against all sorts of 'systems', ancient and modern, biblical or any other; against all kinds of spurious theological certainties. 'They protect these Creeds and Prayers from corruption which scholastic subtlety, sanctioning and organising popular tendencies, have introduced into them, and would introduce again.'[1] The Articles protect us (said Maurice) from any and all 'theological systems'—those varieties of 'magnificent, elaborate perfect machinery of practices, influences, theories, ever contrived or to be contrived . . . for securing the safety of the soul'.[2] 'God's Church cannot be a lifeless stationary thing',[3] and that is what 'systems' would make it. So of the Thirty-nine Articles he could write: 'we crave those Articles for our defence against ancient and modern doctors and their systems; against Cranmer, against Parker, against Davenant, against Laud, against Tillotson, against Warburton, against Dr. Whateley and Dr. Pusey'.[4] 'I look upon [the Articles]', said Maurice, 'as an invaluable charter, protecting us against a system that once enslaved us, and might enslave us again; protecting us also against the systems of the present day—against "Records" and "Times" newspapers, and Bishops of Exeter, and Heads of Houses.'[5]

Now, Maurice is undoubtedly right in distinguishing (as he here does) the Creeds and the Articles. But it may be worth while taking a little further his contrast between the Articles and 'systems', so as to clarify the notion of a tentative theology, and not least its implications for the idea of development in theology.

[1] *Thoughts on the Rule of Conscientious Subscription*, p. 13.
[2] *Ibid.*, p. 25.
[3] *Ibid.*, p. 38.
[4] *Ibid.*, p. ix.
[5] *Life*, i, 399.

The Articles, it will be recalled, were in fact characteristically 'Anglican' reactions at a certain historical period, to certain doctrines—whether 'Protestant' or 'Popish'—which were then controversial and challenging. Undoubtedly, the Articles have to be understood in this complex seventeenth-century context. To this extent the Articles are necessarily contextualized, and to this degree they are 'systematized'. But in being 'reactions' to positions which are for the most part only implicit, there is certainly no intensive systematization and no creation of clear and unambiguous linkages. In this sense, the Articles are very *unsystematic*. In short, for better or worse, the Articles are logically ambiguous. On the one hand, those who framed them certainly believed them to be consistent with Scripture and with the Fathers, in a way in which (they would have said) Protestant and Popish doctrines (however different between themselves) were not. In this way, in being (and in so far as they are) specimens of reliable discourse, they may help teaching and exposition, and can be made (as they often are made to this day) the basis of a systematic exposition of the faith.

On the other hand, they are not given as a series of agreed logical inferences so clear that he who runs may unambiguously read. They have a sufficiently loose fit to conform to various contextual patterns. They were accepted by people as different as a Wilberforce and a Newman. So the Articles at one and the same time both encourage systematization, and make it problematical. This logical ambiguity is only resolved if the Articles are taken to be neither less nor more than they are.

In other words, two conditions alone are necessary, and together they are sufficient, for understanding the Articles:

1. They must be explicitly related to the issues of their own day, out of whose challenge they took their rise.

2. Their connection with Scripture and the Fathers must be explicitly developed.

The trouble is that today, of these two conditions, the first gives the Articles an air of irrelevance, the second an air of obscurantism. The fact is that, historically speaking, the issues and thought-forms of the context in which, for a true understanding, the Articles must necessarily be set, differ enormously from contemporary thought, making their present significance problematical. Nor, secondly, can it be denied that in various ways the links between the Articles and the Scriptures are in need of radical overhaul. The Articles thus seem to many to be both irrelevant for the most part to contemporary issues, and also biblically naive. Yet granted all that, it may still be claimed for the Articles—and no more needs to be claimed—that when set in their historical context, and when linked—whatever the difficulty—with the Scriptures and tradition—they may yet serve to evoke what might be called an 'Anglican attitude'. But the expression of this attitude in terms of contemporary thought would still need working out.

On the whole, then, we may conclude that Maurice was justified in distinguishing between the Articles which can preserve an attitude and be associated with a distinctive devotion, and theological 'systems' which tend to be religious tombs. But, for reasons which will appear presently, it is worth while clarifying yet further Maurice's attitude to systems and the concept of a tentative theology by considering his views on theological development. For in sponsoring the Thirty-nine Articles, Maurice was explicitly accepting one concept of 'development' and rejecting others.

He was certainly objecting to the kind of development which he associated with Tractarians like Ward and (at that time) Newman, a development which sponsored what he viewed as antiquarian additions. He thus criticized the early Newman for an idea of development which was 'most diametrically opposed' to his own, an idea which (he continued) 'would identify *development* and *accumulation*'.[1] Of Ward, he said: 'The accumulation of notions by Fathers, Schoolmen, Mystical writers, not the struggling of living thoughts under these notions, is what captivates him. The bigger the heap, the greater his admiration.'[2] But Maurice was also objecting to a Scholastic view of theological development, which would permit of the elaboration of more and more consistent (or at least not obviously inconsistent) inferences; the construction of an ever larger deductive system. Maurice's objection to both kinds of development was that, in different ways they lost the living God. The 'system' of the one buried him under its pile; the 'system' of the other strangled him by its chains of inference. For Maurice, words might talk of God, but would never embody him, and only succeeded in being currency for God when they perished as they revealed. Doctrinal development was thus matched with 'spiritual' development. In this sense Maurice could (and did) welcome development and to that extent systematization, but it had to be development whose words and phrases were associated with, and patently grounded in a divine disclosure. Maurice was thus led to view every 'system' as a mere chrysalis which perished as a new 'child of promise' emerged as the gift of God. As he himself said: 'Different periods have been overpowered by some one leading thought or conception. The effort to bring this thought to the birth, leads to various observations and experiences of the highest value. It led to the formulation of theories out of those experiences, very diverse and perplexed, but each of certain value. It leads, lastly, to the growth of a system fashioned out of these

[1] *Thoughts on the Rule of Conscientious Subscription*, p. 39.   [2] *Ibid.*, p. 39.

theories and experiences, which becomes a chrysalis' tomb, wherein the child of promise lies till the time when it is destined to emerge.'[1]

Maurice's objections, then, whether to systematic or to 'antiquarian' development, were, we might say, devotional and pastoral: that in fact the larger the 'system' the more it tended to conceal rather than to reveal the light of God, and the more productive of bigotry and prejudice rather than of humility and charity. Perhaps Maurice, being of all his contemporaries the most alert to the logical peculiarities of theological claims and argument, and the most conscious of the constant need to ground theological assertions in a disclosure of God, lest they should become only refined exercises in word-spinning, struggled hardest to reconcile religious devotion and theological uncertainty.

At the risk of trailing a coat and introducing something of a digression, may I suggest that there was, however, one contemporary who, at least in his later days, is perhaps closer to Maurice than he might have supposed, but not closer than many of his critics (I dare say) suspected. This person is Newman.

As Dr. Owen Chadwick has reminded us,[2] Newman in his *Essay on the Development of Christian Doctrine* was elaborating a view which (though he may not have realized it)[3] is, like that of Maurice, in emphatic contrast to the Scholastic view of doctrinal development. On this Scholastic view, doctrinal development proceeds by way of inference, for which the syllogism was supposed to be a model. Development in this sense is logical explication. What was Newman's view? For Newman, 'developments of doctrine are the God-assisted process whereby the Church comes to

[1] *Thoughts on the Rule of Conscientious Subscription*, pp. 38–9.
[2] *From Bossuet to Newman: the Idea of Doctrinal Development.*
[3] See e.g. *loc. cit.* p. 48.

comprehend more fully the structure and the relations of the original revelation, to see round the different aspects of the one idea which she has been given'.[1]

As to this 'idea', Dr. Chadwick comments that at least in this context 'idea' for Newman

does not mean the notion which an individual may form of an object, but the object itself as it is capable of being apprehended in various notions. An idea will in this sense be more complex and many-sided than the individual notions about it, and perhaps never fully 'perceptible' in such notions as human language is capable of expressing. An idea of importance or complexity can only be comprehended in all its aspects through a long period of time and diverse circumstances, which elicit its consequences and its relations. This is what happened in the development of Christian doctrine.[2]

To use an analogy which Newman used on more than one occasion, the Church develops her doctrine as 'a converted soul grows in the true understanding of the faith which at first he apprehends only in broad outline'.[3] More particularly, the 'idea' given by revelation is

like a child's love for its mother . . . deeper and bigger than the words, the 'logic', in which the subject of the experience then or later seeks to describe it. A peasant looks at the sky and is able to prophesy the weather accurately, yet would be unable to satisfy the meteorologist that he possesses sufficient reason for his prophecy. And so religion may contain more truth than theology can describe. 'Mary kept all these sayings and pondered them in her heart.' She received them first: then she reasoned about them. Mary is the type not only of the little child and the peasant, she is the type and model of the theologian and the doctor—and not only of the theologian and doctor, but of the Church herself. The Church first received an impression about which she did not rationalize. And then, in

---

[1] *loc. cit.* p. 149.   [2] *loc. cit.* p. 149.   [3] *loc. cit.* p. 151.

the course of history, she has constructed a theology, doctrines, customs, the offspring of that original impression.[1]

How far is this different from Maurice's view of a 'leading thought or conception' which is eventually brought to birth in some system? True, Maurice does not think of revelation in terms of only *one* idea; nor need we suppose that Maurice and Newman would have given the same account of how the 'system' is fashioned out of the 'idea', or would have accorded the same status to the system when it has emerged. Yet we may think that there are enough similarities between the two to give us cause for interesting speculation.

This is not the place to take much further this comparison between Newman and Maurice. But it is perhaps worth noting that when Maurice prefaced his Warburton lectures on *The Epistle to the Hebrews* with a carefully detailed *Review of Mr. Newman's Theory of Development*, his critique was remarkably sympathetic, and the reader has the impression of many common insights, many points of agreement and, I would even dare say, a common metaphysical concept of authority. Let me exemplify by a few quotations.

Of Newman's concept of an 'idea' Maurice remarks:

I leave him therefore to define ideas as he pleases; and his definition being assumed, I think it is impossible not to be struck with the truth and value of many of the statements which I have quoted. Their eloquence I have been reluctantly forced to weaken, though the reader will detect it even in my abridgement. Nothing, I think, can be more just and striking than his description of the effect of a strong conviction upon a mind which has become possessed with it; how it must work and cannot be let; how it must grow and cannot remain in its first seed; how it must communicate itself to other minds,

[1] *loc. cit.* p. 152.

and be affected by all it finds in them; how spiritual conflicts, and conflicts in the world, the one always answering to the other, must prove its soundness and strength.[1]

Later in the Preface Maurice comments on the conflict between the ecclesiastical parties of his day:

But because God has not been in all our thoughts, one party among us has raised the standard of The Bible, and the other of The Church, as if there were no relation between the two; as if the one did not expound the other; as if the one merely meant a book of opinions delivered centuries ago, and the other a system of opinions existing now. Hence it seems to me have come endless divisions and oppositions which no compromises can adjust, no explanations clear away, until we raise ourselves to a higher point of view, until we in reality, as well as in words, confess that He whom the Bible proclaims as the true King is actually reigning over us. When we believe this truth history kindles into life; there is no portion of it which we wish to pass over; none which we have an interest in perverting. The more good we find everywhere in every direction the more we rejoice; when we see evil in that part which is dearest to us we dare not hide it.[2]

We may compare with this Newman's own words in the *Essay* quoted by Maurice on pp. ix, x of the *Preface*:

There is no aspect such as to go the depth of a real idea; no one term or proposition which can duly and fully represent it; though one representation of it will be more just and appropriate than another; and though when an idea is very complex, it is allowable to consider its different aspects as separate ideas, for the sake of convenience. (p. 34.)

Again,

An attempt has been made to ascertain the 'leading idea', as it has been called, of Christianity; a remarkable essay as

[1] *The Epistle to the Hebrews* (1846), Preface, pp. xii–xiii.
[2] *loc. cit.* pp. cxxv–cxxvi.

directed towards a divine religion, when, even in the existence of the works of man, the task is beyond us. Thus the one idea of the Gospel has been decided by some to be the restoration of our fallen race, by others philanthropy, by others the spirituality of true religious service, by others the salvation of the elect, by others the union of the soul with God. All these representations are truths, as being aspects of Christianity, but none of them is the whole truth. For Christianity has many aspects: it has its imaginative side, its philosophical, its ethical, its political; it is solemn, it is cheerful; it is indulgent, and it is strict; it is light, and it is dark; it is love, and it is fear. (p. 35.)

It is only when Newman claims to find 'an established system' that Maurice hopes that 'the devotion of Mr. Newman's heart' will deliver him 'from this conclusion of his understanding'. But he says regretfully:

I cannot delude myself into the hope that the same will be the issue in all cases. I fear that there are not a few young men who are flying to the belief in an infallible pope, because they have not the courage to ask themselves whether they believe in an Infallible God. The question of our day—we shall find it so more and more—is really between God and Atheism, much more than between Protestantism and Romanism. Let us understand this state of things well; it may make us more reverent and fearful ourselves—more earnest and yet much more gentle of our treatment of others.[1]

So I suggest that both Maurice and Newman recognized that Christian conviction arose as a response to a transcendent authority, and both could speak of this authority as 'infallible'. They differed only in their views as to how this firm conviction was translated into particular assertions and institutions. They differed in this way over 'fact and history'. Maurice and Newman could both characterize the authority as 'given'; but for Maurice this feature

[1] *loc. cit.* p. xliv.

never transferred itself to any 'hypothesis' or 'system'.
Maurice was critical of all translation of conviction into an
authoritative system; whereas Newman believed he had
found, in Maurice's words, 'an established system, not
indeed a dead system, but a living one'.[1] Both were sure
in religion; but differed as to how this certitude showed
itself in theology. Maurice could recognize a kindred
'devotion', though they might differ in the conclusions of
their understandings. Maurice undoubtedly discerned
that, as I have suggested, the Newman of the *Essay* was
fundamentally much closer to him than the Tractarian
Newman, whose heart Maurice may have thought disap-
peared like Ward's beneath an antiquarian accumulation.
We may recall Maurice's concluding remarks in his
Preface:

It seems to me that widely as Mr. Newman's present conclusions are distant from those he once adopted, he has not arrived
at them by any tortuous or illegitimate process. He appears to
have felt strongly twelve years ago, that he was sent into the
world to resist the progress of Rationalism; that the prevalent
English system afforded no barrier against it; that we did
however possess an adequate barrier in the Apostolic constitution, which we had forgotten or made light of; in the books of
the Fathers, which our old divines had held sacred; in the
reverence for sacraments. His voice was heard; numbers of
young men especially felt that he had told them something
which they wanted to know; many believed that the enemy was
subdued. But Mr. Newman finds Rationalism as rampant as
ever; its appearances seem to him not less, but more terrific
than they did at first; the young Englishmen whom he led
have ceased to be satisfied with the defences which he said
were adequate against it; he believes that he must seek for
others which are more impregnable. This course of thought
seems to me a very natural one. I can see nothing in it which

[1] *loc. cit.* p. xlii.

would induce me to disparage the sincerity of the mind which has passed through it. Nor am I much influenced by documents which have been brought forward to prove that Mr. Newman was in heart and feeling a Romanist while he adhered to our communion. Chronology in the history of mental conflicts is most uncertain: today there may be sensations of vehement disgust for that which was once very dear, tomorrow a return of first love. If the decision is ultimately an honest one, we have no right to assume a cognizance of the previous struggles and revulsions of feeling, which are really known only to the Judge of all. I think we shall miss the lesson, the humbling and therefore the useful lesson, which Mr. Newman may teach us, if we busy ourselves in seeking excuses for condemning him. He finds the barriers he thought would preserve us from Rationalism insufficient. Will a mere belief in the Fathers, or in Succession, avail to answer the question, 'Is GOD really among us or no?' Will Sacraments avail, if we look at them apart from Him, if they do not testify of His presence? The Rationalist has gone beneath all visible things, and has asked what is at the ground of them. If we can, in deepest awe, but also with calmness and certainty, give the answer, all forms and orders and visible things will repeat it. We shall see them in a new light; they will have a new meaning for us. We shall satisfy, not stifle, the questioning of others; our own ground will be what it has ever been, but we shall *know* that we are standing on the Rock of Ages.[1]

In so far as Newman's theory of development was essentially God-centred, Maurice could rejoice, and there must be much in Newman's *Essay in aid of a Grammar of Assent* (published in 1870 only two years before Maurice's death) which Maurice might have welcomed. But in any case we begin to see why Maurice (perhaps not as unexpectedly as Dr. Chadwick suggests)[2] greeted Newman's essay 'with gratitude that Newman had now abandoned what he believed to be the rigid antiquarianism of the Tractarian

[1] *loc. cit.* pp. cxxvii–cxxviii.   [2] *From Bossuet to Newman*, p. 164.

doctrine of authority'.[1] It may be that Catholic critics of Newman sensed more clearly than they could formulate, insights into language, a distrust of traditional logic, an empirical historical approach to 'development' and a concept of a tentative theology which were as ill-fitting for their traditional apologetic, as they well matched the sympathies of Maurice. Yet it was perhaps because of these very insights which Newman shared with Maurice that, in Dr. Chadwick's words, 'Newman contributed more than any other Catholic' to enabling 'a conservative society' to refuse 'to follow several seductive proposals' which would have led towards absolute obscurantism'.[2]

Let us now turn to link these reflections on 'system' and doctrinal development with the practice of Subscription and Assent to theological formularies such as the Thirty-nine Articles. Clergymen, as we have noted, are not only required to 'assent' to the Thirty-nine Articles, but also (it will be recalled) to the Book of Common Prayer and to the Ordering of Bishops, Priests and Deacons. What sort of 'assent' is it that can be given to all three? Is it a sort of 'nodding assent', merely acknowledging (so to say) the presence of this specifically Anglican furniture in the large room in which our feet are set? No. Subscription—'subscription', i.e. the pledging of ourselves by our very name —is directed to the claim that 'such doctrine as the Articles set forth' is 'agreeable to the Word of God'. Which means that Anglicans assent to these Articles as forming with the Creeds and Scripture and the Prayer Book, guides for reliable assertions about that with which we are confronted in God's disclosure of himself in Jesus Christ.

Subscription must then have a two-fold character: (i) It must be to *formulae in a context*. The 'general' or 'full' sense of the Thirty-nine Articles is no pick-and-choose

---

[1] *loc. cit.* Preface, pp. x, xi.   [2] *loc. cit.* Preface, p. x.

assent, no vague or loose assent, but an assent to the Articles which acknowledges that for their 'meanings' we embody them not only in a wider context of Scripture and tradition but also in the context of the specific historical issues in relation to which they emerged. (ii) In this way Subscription becomes a declaration *ex animo* of personal sympathy with an 'Anglican attitude' that these Articles in these contexts express and evoke. So we solve the moral and intellectual problem of subscription by affirming verbal formulae which are only 'understood' when (*a*) they are linked unambiguously through the Creeds with the Scriptures and (*b*) in this way succeed in being evocative of Christian devotion, in which (*c*) are then grounded contemporary Christian judgments and the possibility of genuine theological development.

For, in the words of Maurice which we have already quoted, 'God's Church cannot be a lifeless, stationary thing.'[1] No more can theology. The only test therefore of a genuine subscription is what happens afterwards: we must see what a man does and says while developing his theological discourse. *Ex animo* subscription commits us to one thing only—perpetual development, and it is this alone which justifies us in subscribing *ex animo* while being tentative in theology.

So subscription to the Articles and similar formulae, is much more like an affirmation of personal loyalty, which the years ever enrich, than it is like 'signing on the dotted line', which we do as a tax-declarer, form-filler or licence-holder, and where personal, metaphysical affirmations are glaringly inappropriate. Nor, from what I have said above need I apologize for taking Newman's analogy to explicate a position suggested by Maurice. It follows on this analogy that to be too keen on subscription or formulae, and to

[1] *Thoughts on the Rule of Conscientious Subscription*, p. 38.

G

interpret both on a legalistic or form-filling model is to misunderstand what Christian faith and love is.[1] The boy who continually requests of his girl-friend, 'Darling, *do* tell me that you love me', is hardly likely to have found his wife. Rather do we look for a single profession which declares a loyalty which it is a lifetime's business to work out. A church which is too interested in Subscription is like the mistaken lover. What the Church can and must do, however, is to sponsor relentlessly the development of the context of the Articles, past and present; recognizing, however, that the day when the clothes exactly fit will be the day when we arrive in heaven, and need neither theology nor assent to Articles.

This leads us to a question topical in our own time and a question whose discussion may help to elucidate further the concept of a tentative theology and the idea of theological development. What about a revision of the Articles? Must this not be both possible and desirable? What sort of answers to this question are suggested by our views on development? Our earlier discussion suggests, I think, that we must distinguish between two kinds of 'revision':

1. Revision may be called for because, as we have already hinted, the links between the Articles on the one hand and the Creeds and Scriptures on the other need an overhaul. It would certainly be rather surprising if the growth of our knowledge about the Creeds and about the Bible together with our contemporary insights into religious language did not demand some revision here.

[1] It was this (as he held) *mis*understanding of, and *mis*use of Subscription which led Maurice to be later (1853) critical of Subscription to the Articles (see *Life*, ii, 154). For the full picture, however, we must remember that as late as 1870 he said of *Subscription No Bondage*: 'No book which I have written expresses more strongly what then were, and still are, my deepest convictions' (*Life*, i, 174).

But how useful is a revision of this kind going to be? What result in fact would such a revision have? The result could only be (at best) to produce the kind of Articles which Churchmen of the sixteenth century might have framed in response to challenges of their day if they had been equipped with a mid-twentieth-century honours degree in theology. Even if such Articles could be framed, it would seem that they would inevitably possess a curiously mongrel, anachronistic character and they would certainly be of very little use. How many of our problems today are those of four hundred years ago?

2. So when 'revision' of the Articles is called for, it is generally a revision which would be directed to the intellectual challenge of our own day. It is then not so much a 'revision' of old Articles which is being asked for, as a formulation of new ones. On the other hand it might be said that these new Articles might be produced one by one, by bringing the present Articles into contact with contemporary thought, biblical and philosophical, probing and resolving apparent conflicts and in effect translating the 'Anglican attitude' into contemporary terms. The result would then be to supply us with some reliable guides —one stage beyond Credal affirmations—for the development of Christian discourse in our own day. Should not new Articles be devised in this way to meet the challenge of our times in a way in which our present Articles met the challenge of a past day?

This seems a very persuasive suggestion, but I do not think the parallel holds. When our Articles were devised there was an agreed approach to the Bible, and even the controversies which provoked them arose within a broad common culture. Today, the position is quite otherwise. By contrast, over a hundred years of the historical and critical study of the Bible have led to no agreed perspective on it, let alone conclusions.[1] Further, some of the most threatening of the intellectual battles the Christian has to fight are not from within but from the outside, and being not only cosmological but epistemological, even penetrate far enough to raise serious difficulties about the kind of appeal which Christians make or might wish to make to the Bible. Faced by these complex and intricate critical issues, what is needed is not more Articles, but much more preliminary under-labouring, much more spadework.

In the case of controversies between Christians, the primary need is to trace back our assertions about (say) episcopacy or inter-communion to their source and ground, to discover how and in what way we can (if we can) claim that these key-assertions disclose God-in-Christ. This is something far more difficult, far less spectacular and far less exciting than flag-waving. But it is a *sine qua non* for any genuine Christian dialogue and fruitful controversy, and it has the additional merit that if practised it would help us to learn afresh what are patterns of reliable Christian argument.

In the case of controversies arising from outside the Christian faith the first need is to understand and measure the challenge, to see e.g. where contemporary theories of man and the universe impinge on Christian doctrine, and where frontier contacts and frontier incidents occur. Here the first need is for patience and humility: only on that condition have we any hope of ultimately reformulating an adequate and reliable Christian world-view.

The primary need is then for immense charity and immense frankness, honest declaration of uncertainties, confession of perplexities, admission of inconsistencies and errors. Let everyone try to say quite explicitly where the

[1] There are of course some biblical theologians who would claim to see the end of the tunnel.

shoe pinches. We might perhaps begin by seeing where people have trouble with the Articles; what questions they provoke; where they seem to come into conflict with contemporary ideas; where they fail to give reliable guidance.

But can we eventually hope for another set of Articles expressive (say) of the 'Anglican attitude'? I doubt it: for many of the issues—those concerned with the possibility and character of reliable Christian reasoning—could plainly never have answers in Article form; and we may doubt whether satisfactory and reliable tabloid answers could be framed in the case of other controversies either.

There would also arise another difficulty if new Articles were ever formulated as a kind of revised syllabus of systematic theology. It may be (and Maurice would say with some plausibility that it is) the case that when our present Articles are appropriately contextualized, they can evoke a specifically Anglican attitude; though many would say that a better expression of the Anglican attitude is to be found in the Prayer Book. Be that as it may, the great danger of any future Articles designed to meet far-ranging and diverse difficulties of the kind that confront us today, is that they would, like Maurice's 'systems', cramp and destroy religious life, thought and worship. Speaking of the 'systems' of his day he remarks:

The Romanist's is round and smooth, the Protestant's irregular, jagged, broken. Evidently the one is a master of his art, the other is a blunderer, knows very little about it, yet will be continually making the attempt. Nor is it different, I conceive, with the Englishman. He, too, is most clumsy at this work: he builds towers, but they fall down—God comes down to confound the labour and the tongues of those who are engaged in it. Each new attempt at the creation of a system leads to new divisions and parties. A disheartening result indeed, if this is the task men are sent into the world to perform; if, without a system, we can have no religion, no theological science, no Church. But if religious feeling, exercises, life, have been cramped and destroyed by the bondage of system; if system in every department has been the plague of science, making it, not the knowledge of that which is, but merely an aggregate of human conceptions; if therefore it has been especially the curse of theological science, which is grounded on the Revelation of Him who is and was and is to come, and which should be ever exhibiting His revealed Name in some new aspect, as interpreting some new aspect in human history; if, lastly, a system in all ages has been hiding the Church from view, making it assume the character of a school or a sect, destroying its reality, robbing it of its Centre, then thanks be to God that we are reminded by so many proofs how vain it is for us to mould a system, call it Protestant, Anglican, Catholic, what you like; how needful it is for us to use the faculties which have been given to us in some other direction; to be content, if we can, to dwell in a house not made with hands, without caring to raise one.[1]

Sobered by such reflections, we might say that if anyone is looking for new 'Articles', why look further than the Bible and the Creeds? Have not these for our own day something of the significance which Maurice assigned to the Thirty-nine Articles? Here, whether in the Epistles or the Creeds, are the first understandings of the Christian gospel, the first attempts at consistency, at some measure of systematization. The Bible and the Creeds unite all Christians in the way in which Maurice believed that the Articles enshrined a basis for unity between Anglicans and Dissenters:

> The Articles then, I conceive, are no hindrance to Dissenters uniting with us, or with one another; but the more we become acquainted with their meaning and spirit, the more we shall be able to feel ourselves, and to shew them, what the grounds of

[1] *Epistle to the Hebrews*, pp. cxxi–cxxii.

unity and fellowship are, the more we shall be able to meet each person on the ground of the doctrine which has been revealed to him, and shew him that this doctrine forms an integral portion of our own faith.[1]

This is of course not to deny that there are differences, and important differences, between the Creeds and the Articles. The Creeds are the first and classic essay in consistency and give us rules to guide all subsequent discourse; whereas the Articles can be seen as specimen discourse designed and developed to help teaching and exposition in certain historical circumstances. Creeds and Articles are different in so far as they may be roughly compared in particular to the rules of the game, and the game itself. But our position today is that we are perplexed about the meaning of the rules, and need to discover what sorts of game are permissible. Our difficulty today is not so much with conflicting claims, not so much with different games, as to see how this diversity arises from and can be routed back to a Christian disclosure. Which means that our first task must be to elucidate the logic of Bible and Creeds, learning afresh how to talk as Christians, and how to talk reliably.

So it would seem that, so far as the Thirty-nine Articles go, the difficulties to which they lead suggest neither their revision nor their replacement. At best they are a not unambiguous declaration of the Anglican attitude. But we might think that the sooner the Church of England asks only for such assent to them as is appropriate to their character, the better. It is not the Articles as much as Subscription that calls for revision.

At the moment, like a dog whining as it smells smoke, or a door creaking from the flames within the room it keeps closed, the Articles may disturb us by being theological

[1] *Subscription No Bondage*, p. 115.

irritants. But once we are roused, and have acknowledged the useful significance of dog or door, our urgent duty is to enter the blazing room to save what we can of our most treasured possessions. So must our concern today be not so much with creaking Articles as with the treasure they were designed to enclose, which means that our first concern must be with the Scriptures and with Creeds as pre-conditions for all reliable Christian discourse. Yet I must not be taken to imply that this concern with Scripture and the Creeds will have to be completed before Christian theology begins to be developed—for in elucidating the logic of Bible and Creeds, in learning how to talk, we will talk, and talk theologically. But what character will that theology, that theological talking, have? We return in the end to the question which has been behind our discussion the whole time.

What have we learnt about the character of a tentative theology from considering the Articles and subscription, and the idea of development in doctrine? What have we learnt about the way in which we may, and must be, tentative in theology? The great lesson we have to learn, and the lesson which Maurice abundantly teaches is that we must recognize on the one hand the limitations, the partial character, the broad contextual setting of all our Christian assertions and on the other hand their necessary grounding in God, their fulfilment in devotion. If we may try briefly to epitomize Maurice's teaching it is that theology 'cannot be a lifeless stationary thing'[1] precisely because its topic, God, is God 'of whom words may speak', but whom they cannot 'embody'.[2] For the same reason theology will never be kept within the tight confines of a deductive system but in one way and another it will always display a variety of reliable discourse, varied too in its

[1] See pp. 37, 69 and 81 above.   [2] See pp. 29 and 67 above.

degrees of reliability. As we learn to be articulate in theology, we must at every point be sensitive and critical about
our assertions—sensitive to discern how they arise out of,
and must consequently be referred for their elucidation to,
Christian disclosures; critically aware of their logical peculiarities and partial character. What we have to learn is the
thrill of theological exploration, the delight of theological
discovery, a rhythm of faith and love with understanding.
It is this we must substitute for a be-all and end-all
theology, for theological certainties and infallibilities. We
must learn to be sure, to give *ex animo* assent when we can
do no other, while all the time being theologically tentative.
Commitment is only a synonym for credulity, prejudice
and bigotry; subscription is only the label for a closed
mind, if we suppose ourselves to have found a complete
and final map of that which called forth our commitment.
If someone now protests: but surely the doctrine of the
Trinity (for example) cannot be open to revision, the
question to ask in reply is: what *is* the doctrine of the
Trinity? It is no descriptive label for the Christian's God;
revision is not a matter of getting a better label for the
facts. Rather is Trinitarian belief a Trinitarian-directed
inquiry which shall ever broaden its scope and its setting
backwards and forwards. So the old ethical problem of
subscription again disappears and we can repeat Benjamin
Whichcote's maxim: 'He that never changed any of his
opinions, never corrected any of his mistakes; and he who
was never wise enough to find out any mistakes in himself,
will not be charitable enough to excuse what he reckons
mistakes in others.'[1]

---

[1] No. 53. *Moral and Religious Aphorisms collected from the Manuscript papers
of the reverend and learned doctor Whichcote*, ed. Dr. J. Jeffery (1703) and
re-edited by Dr. S. Salter (1753). Aphorism 53 in this expanded form is
only in the 1753 edition.

My point then is that we are to be tentative, but always contextually tentative, about our theology, while grounding that theology in a disclosure of God. In this way we are to be sure in religion while being tentative, but contextually tentative in theology. This means that at each stage, the tentative is controlled by the context to date, so that we always assert something firmly and squarely in a context. But such assertions are always ripe for development. This development must link any new assertion ever more coherently with the Creeds and Scriptures, and lead us to a greater comprehensiveness in so far as that new assertion will presumably match up better to a variety of contemporary challenges. So to be justly tentative in theology is to build continuously on an ever-changing context of *pro tem.* certainty and to have the humility which, while it strives energetically to build from such a base the best theological map it can, recognizes that it will *never* succeed in 'embodying' the Mystery. A contextually tentative theology is not a euphemism for scepticism; nor does it suppose that all theologies are equally good; nor is it an excuse for sloth and ignorance. It is rather an apt counterpart to our vision of God, and Maurice is to be honoured for insisting on these themes in a day when the prospect was less relished, and its sponsorship more precarious than it is today. We are learning better to be as frank with friends as with opponents, and to be as charitable to opponents as to friends.

INDEX

Biblical References